Generations
Of Cooking

A Cookbook Celebrating

*the **Fortieth Anniversary** of*

Girl Scouts of Shawnee Council, Inc.

Generations Of Cooking
A Cookbook Celebrating the Fortieth Anniversary of Girl Scouts of Shawnee Council, Inc.

Published by Girl Scouts of Shawnee Council, Inc.

Copyright © 2003 by
Girl Scouts of Shawnee Council, Inc.

ISBN: 0-9726507-0-9

Edited, Designed, and Manufactured by

CommunityClassics™

An imprint of
FRP
P.O. Box 305142
Nashville, Tennessee 37230
(800) 358-0560

Manufactured in the United States of America
First Printing: 2003
4,000 copies

Mission Statement

Girl Scouts of Shawnee Council, Inc., is an informal, educational, spiritually based, value-oriented organization. Shawnee Council emphasizes the diverse needs and interests of today's girls and adult role models while stressing service, developing self-esteem, and preparing girls for the future.

Table of Contents

Acknowledgments

Sincere appreciation and thanks to the following individuals who helped make this far-fetched idea a reality.

Ora Dixon, *President* Dee Covey, *Chief Executive Officer*

Committee

Dr. Sally Pepper, D.V.M.
Board Member-at-Large

Mary Ann Jenkins
Board Member-at-Large

Marguerite Cyr
First President

Mary Bourdeau
Second Vice President

Nicole DeGrave
Board Member-at-Large

Elaine Dorosh
Former Staff Member

Staff Members

Pamela Allen
Registrar

Sandy Jones
Resource Alumna Executive

Fran Russ
Director of Product Sales

Carol Diehl
Director of Program Services

Rachael Lewis
Business Assistant

Davida Mosby
Administrative Assistant

A very special thanks to Mrs. Marguerite Cyr for the drawing on the front cover.

We would also like to thank Brownie Troop 595 for submitting many recipes from which to choose.

Preface

Whether it's toasting marshmallows at a campfire or sampling ethnic delicacies, Girl Scouting has been cooking up good things for girls in Shawnee Council since 1963. Girl Scouting is concerned about good nutrition and health, but also about the fun and friendship that comes from sharing and learning together.

As you look through this special cookbook, you may be reminded of your first adventure in cooking or the first time you realized that a friend's family had some favorite food you had never tasted or even heard of. Those memories are part of what Girl Scouting is all about, and all those who have contributed to this book are helping to shape more good memories for tomorrow.

These Girl Scout recipes, like Girl Scout people, are many and varied and full of surprises. As you use this cookbook, you may rediscover some old favorites, but be sure to take advantage of new ones, too, as you celebrate the food, friendship, and Fortieth Anniversary of Girl Scouts of Shawnee Council and honor the woman, Marguerite Cyr, Shawnee Council's first President.

Dee Covey

Chief Executive Officer

The Girl Scout Promise

On my honor, I will try:
To serve God and my country,
To help people at all times,
And to live by the Girl Scout Law.

Dedication

Marguerite E. Cyr

A short while ago, my mother, Marguerite Cyr, and I were visiting when she brought out a small box of memories to share. Carefully tucked inside the box were her Girl Scout pins, merit badges, and membership cards from her days as a Girl Scout. It was this early involvement in Girl Scouting that started my Mom on a lifelong path of community service and giving of her time and talents to those in her life.

A lifetime member of the Girl Scouts, Mom's terms as troop leader and as a member of the Board of Directors of the Girl Scout Council of Hagerstown were followed by her involvement in the creation of the Shawnee Girl Scout Council. As President, she oversaw the council those first years from 1963 to 1966.

After stepping down from the Presidency, Mom again served as Board Member and remains involved today, assisting in areas where her expertise and talents are most useful. In 2000, the Shawnee Girl Scout Council honored Mom by establishing the Marguerite E. Cyr Award, which is awarded to individuals who have shown outstanding leadership to both the council and the community.

Concurrent with her involvement in the Girl Scouts, Mom became active in the Red Cross. As a member of the Board of Directors from 1965 to 1992, she served as Chapter Chairman and on various committees before becoming an Honorary Member of the Board of Directors in 1992.

In recognition of her contributions, Mom was awarded the Beulah T. Meyers Award in 1985, the Clara Barton Certificate in 1992, and received her 35-year Service Award in 2000. As with the Girl Scouts, she remains close to the organization and to the friends she has made through her involvement.

Active in the local art community, Mom is a member of the Valley Art Association, the Mansion House Gallery, the YMCA Wednesday Portrait Workshop, and the Spectrum Seven, a group of seven local women artists. An ongoing contributor to local art shows, she held her own One Woman Show in 1993. Today, Mom is a Docent at the Washington County Fine Art Museum, volunteering as a guide to visitors to the museum.

It is quite an honor for the Girl Scouts of Shawnee Council to dedicate this cookbook to our Mother in recognition of her contributions and involvement over the years.

In gathering my thoughts to make this introduction, I am again reminded that Mom has kept the Girl Scout Law close to her heart: always doing her best, being fair and honest, helping where needed, being friendly and considerate, improving the world around her, and showing respect for herself and others. In return, she has won the love and respect of her many friends and her community.

Our family is happy and proud that this cookbook is dedicated to Marguerite E. Cyr, our Mom. We hope that you find many recipes that become your favorites.

Laura C. Cyr-Varadi

Foreword

It gives me great pleasure to present *Generations of Cooking*.

Are you selecting good food choices for a healthy lifestyle? We create our own state of wellness each day by being responsible for our own health or bringing peace into our life. The food that we eat, the thoughts we think, the emotions that we feel and believe all have a very important impact on our health, happiness, and wholeness of life. So being in control of our lives involves choices of good eating habits.

Each day that we fail to deal effectively with the stresses of life we are drawn closer to illness. With the proper diet, appropriate exercise patterns, and developing more of a positive attitude, illnesses can be prevented and in many cases overcome.

So, a correct diet, exercise, and a commitment to life all have enormous and positive effects on health. Being healthy alone cannot be emphasized only, but we must have a sense of wholeness as we relate to one another and to our common creator. Given these choices, what's so magical about another cookbook?

This cookbook is magical because it is a way to celebrate our mission through education and fun for all of us and one of many projects that we have undertaken to celebrate our Fortieth Anniversary and the Council's rewarding future.

The Girl Scout Law

I will do my best to be
honest and fair, friendly and helpful,
considerate and caring, courageous and strong, and
responsible for what I say and do.
and to respect myself and others, respect authority,
use resources wisely, make the world a better place,
and be a sister to every Girl Scout.

The recipes are special and submitted with love and pride from our families and friends across the Council. Many of these recipes are family favorites and are prepared for those very meaningful family occasions and outings. As you page through this cookbook, you will encounter recipes that will bring back fond memories of your Girl Scout experiences or perhaps that of family members involved in outdoor activities, camping, and just enjoying nature.

The uniqueness of the cookbook layout is illustrated from the Girl Scouts of the Shawnee Council's history to our tips and favorite tidbits on camping offers the essence of Girl Scouting past and future.

Please join with us for all of our special anniversary celebrations and planning for a promising future ahead. It is our prayer that you will cultivate a continuous relationship of financial support for Girl Scouting, involving the people around you to do the same and receive a blessing about life in general in the process. With your financial support, we will be able to provide a significant increase in services to girls everywhere throughout multicultural communities at the local level and maintain our presence in this preeminent organization for girls at the national level providing *Girl Scouting to every girl everywhere.*

Ora W. Dixon

President

History of Shawnee Council

In 1963, under the guidance of the Girls Scouts of the USA, Shawnee Council as we know it was formed by a merger of local councils: Blue Ridge Council in Virginia, Eastern Panhandle Council in Eastern West Virginia, Washington County, Maryland; Shawnee Council in Allegany County, Maryland; Garrett County, West Virginia; and Bedford County in Pennsylvania. This was a time when councils all over the country were merging to provide more efficient services and greater uses of resources. In 1999, the name of the council was changed to The Girl Scouts of Shawnee Council.

At the time of the merger, the main office was located in Cumberland, Maryland. The other three offices were maintained as field offices. For many years, each continued to function independently, providing its own program materials, camping activities, and troop support. In 1972, under the guidance of the Girl Scouts of the USA and recommendation of the Board of Directors, the central office was moved from Green Street in Cumberland, Maryland, to Porter Avenue in Martinsburg, West Virginia. In the same year, the out-based offices were closed. In 1977, R.E. Lutz of Martinsburg donated land to Shawnee Council at 1602 Edwin Miller Boulevard, Martinsburg, West Virginia, to build an office. Construction on the office began in April of 1978. In September of 1978, the building was completed and the office was then moved to the new location. In 1999, the address changed to 153 McMillan Court, Martinsburg, West Virginia. In 1975, the council adopted Project G.I.R.L.S., a plan to develop a conference center, office, and camp in Hancock, Maryland.

The camps owned by Shawnee were Camp White Rock, Capon Bridge, West Virginia; Tioga, Cumberland, Maryland; Pine Ridge, Glengary, West Virginia; and CoHeLo, Hagerstown, Maryland. In 1976, the Hancock site proved unfeasible and the Board took action to sell three of the camps owned by Shawnee and develop Camp White Rock. This camp is the most central resident camp for Shawnee Council. White Rock was purchased from Mrs. Virginia Grimm on June 13, 1952, by Blue Ridge Girl Scout Council, Winchester, Virginia, for $11,000. Mr. Eugene Cooper named Camp White Rock for the big white rock on the west side of the river. The Cooper cabin was purchased for $500. The original cabin was taken down, but the fireplace was left and the current Cooper building was built around it.

This building was known as Chinkapin until 1993, when the building was rededicated in honor of the Cooper family, the original owners. In 1961, Dudley Hall, the kitchen and dining hall, was built. It was named for Dudley Lichlider who lived in Winchester, Virginia. Mr. Lichlider volunteered many hours helping to purchase and build Camp White Rock. Camp White Rock is comprised of 119 acres in the main camp area; 19 acres of undeveloped triangular plot across Christian Church Road from the camp entrance. In 1978, Riverview was purchased from Russell B. Oates and is comprised of 15 acres, located across the creek from Cooper Lodge. Riverview got its name from a contest where the membership of Shawnee Council submitted names. The other units were named for Robin Hood: Sherwood for the forest, Hemlock and Dogwood for trees found in the forest, Bluff because it overlooks the Cacapon River from a bluff, and Pioneer for the early settlers.

In the 1980s, Girl Scout Service Centers (out-based offices) were opened to better serve the volunteers. They are currently located in Moorefield, West Virginia; Cumberland, Maryland; Hagerstown, Maryland; and Winchester, Virginia. In 1985, the council began operation of Shawnee Council Shoppe (an official equipment agency) to serve the needs of the girls and volunteers. In 1990, Shawnee sponsored a Girl Scout National Wider Opportunity, Pedal Pushers. There were 50 participants and 8 adults from 36 states, including Alaska and Hawaii. One participant was vision impaired. The challenge was met by using a tandem bike. These participants biked the C & O Canal from Cumberland, Maryland, to Georgetown, Maryland, then spent the 4th of July on the Washington Mall. In 1993, an Archives Department was started at Shawnee. The purpose is to preserve Girl Scouting of Shawnee Council and GSUSA.

In 1993, cabins were donated to replace staff row at Camp White Rock. In 2001, a campaign was launched to have cabins donated to replace all but one of the units at Camp White Rock. At present there have been 13 cabins donated; four have been built. A dedication was held in April of 2002 for the cabins constructed and donated. In 1997, the new Nature Center was dedicated in honor of James Hewitt. This building replaced an existing Nature Lodge. From 1999-2002, several Day of Caring United Way projects have been donated, a pond was built, a shelter erected, and improvements to the council office have been completed.

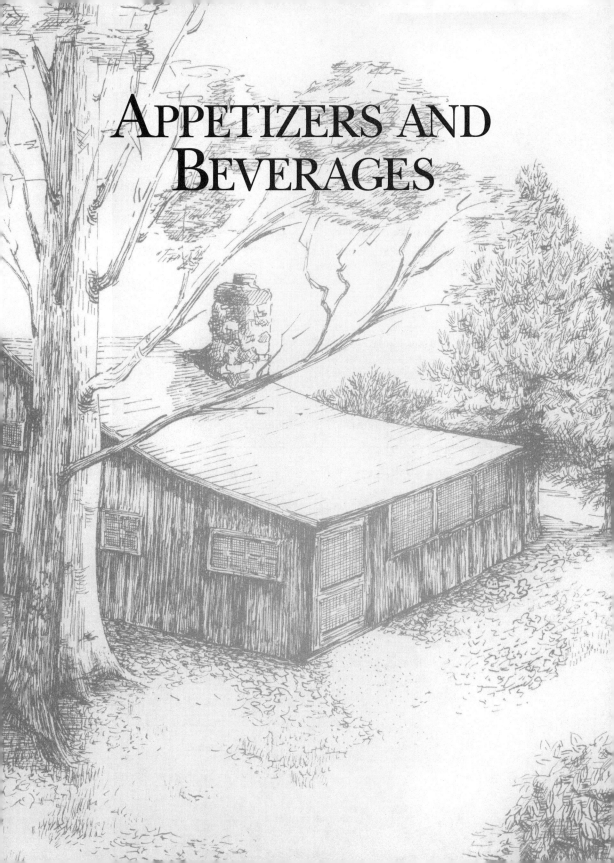

APPETIZERS AND BEVERAGES

Helpful Hints

When your hands are badly stained from gardening, add a teaspoon of sugar to the soapy lather you wash them in.

Use paper cups as handy containers for your "drippings" in the refrigerator as they take up little room and can be thrown away when empty.

Before emptying the bag of your vacuum cleaner on a newspaper, sprinkle water on it and there will be no scattering of dust.

Keep a toothbrush at the kitchen sink— you will find it useful for cleaning rotary beaters, graters, choppers, and similar utensils.

To remove burned-on starch from your iron, sprinkle salt on a sheet of waxed paper and slide the iron back and forth on it several times. Then polish with silver polish until roughness or stain is removed.

Plant a few sprigs of dill near your tomato plants to prevent tomato worms on the plants.

Marigolds will prevent rodents.

Spray garbage bags with ammonia to prevent dogs from tearing into the bags before they are picked up.

You can clean darkened aluminum pans easily by boiling them in two teaspoons of cream of tartar dissolved in a quart of water. Ten minutes will do it.

If a cracked dish is boiled in sweet milk for 45 minutes, the crack will be so welded together that it will hardly be visible and will be so strong that it will withstand the same usage as before.

To drip-dry a garment faster and with fewer wrinkles, hang garment over the top of a dry cleaner's plastic bag.

Remove the odor from your hands after cutting onions by simply washing them with fresh lemon juice, salt, or baking soda.

Exercise patience when making gravy. Sift the flour and sing as you stir so the time will pass quickly.

When making chicken and dumplings, always drop the dough strips into the pot while the chicken and broth are boiling. Do not stir the dumplings until they are almost tender.

A dash of baking powder added to mashed potatoes will make them fluffy and light.

Tex-Mex Layered Appetizer

2 cans jalapeño bean dip
3 medium avocados, mashed
$1/2$ teaspoon salt
$1/4$ teaspoon pepper
1 cup sour cream
1 envelope taco seasoning mix
8 ounces (2 cups) shredded Cheddar cheese
1 can black olives, chopped
1 bunch green onions including tops, chopped
3 medium tomatoes, chopped

Spread the bean dip over the bottom of a large platter. Spread the avocados over the bean dip. Sprinkle with the salt and pepper.

Combine the sour cream and taco seasoning mix in a bowl and mix well. Spread over the avocados. Layer with the cheese, black olives, green onions and tomatoes. Serve with tortilla chips.

Yield: 10 to 15 servings

Note: This recipe would work as a full meal.

NO RACE CAN PROSPER TILL IT LEARNS THERE IS AS MUCH DIGNITY IN TILLING A FIELD AS IN WRITING A POEM.

—Booker T. Washington

Shrimp Dip

1 (5-ounce) can deveined shrimp
1/2 cup mayonnaise
1/2 cup sour cream
1/4 cup cocktail sauce

Rinse the shrimp and drain well. Chop the shrimp. Combine the mayonnaise, sour cream and cocktail sauce in a bowl and mix well. Stir in the shrimp. Chill until serving time. Serve with dip-style corn chips.

Yield: 8 to 10 servings

Artichoke Dip

8 ounces cream cheese, softened, cut into cubes
1 cup mayonnaise
1 cup sour cream
1 cup grated Parmesan cheese
1 (14-ounce) can artichoke hearts, drained and chopped
1 garlic clove, pressed
1 teaspoon dill weed
1/8 teaspoon salt

Combine the cream cheese, mayonnaise, sour cream, Parmesan cheese, artichokes, garlic, dill weed and salt in a food processor. Process for 1 to 2 minutes or until blended. Spoon into a greased baking dish. Bake at 375 degrees for 45 to 60 minutes or until golden brown. Serve with pita chips or bread slices.

Yield: 6 to 8 servings

Salsa with Cilantro

1 pound Roma or Italian tomatoes (about 10)
1/2 cup finely chopped red onion
1/2 to 3/4 cup finely chopped fresh cilantro
1 garlic clove, minced
1 large jalapeño chile, or 2 small jalapeño chiles, seeded and deveined
1 tablespoon extra-virgin olive oil
Juice of 1 lime
Salt and pepper to taste

Combine the tomatoes, onion, cilantro, garlic, jalapeño chile, olive oil, lime juice, salt and pepper in a bowl and mix well. Let stand at room temperature until serving time.

Yield: 10 to 15 servings

Chutney Cheese Spread

1 cup (4 ounces) shredded Cheddar cheese
3 ounces cream cheese, softened
2 to 3 tablespoons sherry
1 tablespoon curry powder
Major Grey's chutney
Chopped green onions

Combine the Cheddar cheese, cream cheese, sherry and curry powder in a bowl and mix well. Shape into a ball. Place on a serving plate. Chill, covered, until serving time. Top with Major Grey's chutney and sprinkle with chopped green onions. Serve with crackers.

Yield: 8 servings

Cheese Ball

16 ounces cream cheese, softened
1 small can crushed pineapple, drained
1/4 cup finely chopped green bell pepper
1 tablespoon finely chopped onion
1 cup pecan pieces

Combine the cream cheese, pineapple, bell pepper and onion in a
bowl and mix well. Shape into a ball using waxed paper. Coat with the
pecans. Place on a serving plate. Chill, covered, until serving time.
Serve with crackers.

Yield: 15 to 20 servings

Pineapple Cheese Ball

16 ounces cream cheese, softened
1 (8-ounce) can crushed pineapple, drained
1 cup chopped pecans
1 cup finely chopped dried beef
1/4 cup finely chopped green bell pepper
2 tablespoons finely chopped onion
1 tablespoon seasoned salt
1/2 to 1 cup chopped pecans
Chopped fresh parsley

Beat the cream cheese in a large mixing bowl. Add the pineapple,
1 cup pecans, dried beef, bell pepper, onion and seasoned salt gradually,
beating constantly. Shape into a ball. Coat with 1/2 to 1 cup pecans and
parsley. Place on a serving plate. Chill, covered, until serving time.

Yield: 15 to 20 servings

Cheese Ring

16 ounces sharp Cheddar cheese, shredded
16 ounces mild Cheddar cheese, shredded
1 cup mayonnaise
1 or 2 garlic cloves
1 small sweet onion, minced
1 to 2 teaspoons cayenne pepper
Pecan halves
Fresh strawberries or cherries
1 jar strawberry jam

Combine the cheese, mayonnaise, garlic, onion and cayenne pepper in a bowl and mix well.

Line a tube pan with plastic wrap. Spoon the cheese mixture into the tube pan, tapping the pan to firmly pack the cheese mixture. Chill, covered with plastic wrap, until serving time.

Invert the cheese ring onto a large round platter. Remove the plastic wrap. Decorate the top of the cheese ring with pecan halves and strawberries. Garnish the outside rim of the cheese ring with fresh parsley sprigs. Spoon the strawberry jam into the center of the cheese ring. Serve with Town House Crackers or Ritz Crackers.

Yield: 20 to 25 servings

ALL OUR DREAMS CAN COME TRUE—IF WE HAVE THE

COURAGE TO PURSUE THEM.

—Walt Disney

Salmon Ball

1 (15-ounce) can salmon, drained and flaked
8 ounces cream cheese, softened
1/2 cup chopped pecans
2 tablespoons lemon juice
1 tablespoon prepared horseradish
1/4 teaspoon salt
1/4 cup chopped fresh parsley

Combine the salmon, cream cheese, pecans, lemon juice, horseradish and salt in a bowl and mix well. Chill, covered, in the refrigerator. Shape into a ball. Coat with the parsley. Serve with assorted crackers.

Yield: 1 (6-inch) ball

Pepper Jelly

6 small hot peppers (about 1/4 cup)
1 1/2 cups chopped green bell peppers
1/2 cup vinegar
6 cups sugar
1 cup vinegar
1 bottle CERTO Liquid Fruit Pectin
Green food coloring (optional)

Chop the hot peppers. Combine the hot peppers, bell peppers and 1/2 cup vinegar in a blender. Process until well mixed. Combine the pepper mixture, sugar, 1 cup vinegar and fruit pectin in a saucepan. Bring to a boil, stirring frequently. Remove from the heat. Stir in food coloring. Ladle into six hot sterilized 1/2-pint jars, leaving 1/2 inch headspace. Chill, covered with waxed paper, until serving time. Serve over blocks of cream cheese.

Yield: 6 (1/2-pint) jars

Chicken Liver Pâté

Butter
1 pound chicken livers
3 tablespoons mayonnaise or mayonnaise-type salad dressing
2 tablespoons lemon juice
2 tablespoons butter or margarine, softened
1 tablespoon minced onion
1/2 teaspoon dry mustard
1/2 teaspoon salt
Dash of pepper
8 to 10 drops of hot pepper sauce (optional)

Melt a small amount of butter in a saucepan. Add the chicken livers. Cook, covered, until the livers are no longer pink, stirring occasionally. Press through a food mill.

Combine the chicken livers, mayonnaise, lemon juice, 2 tablespoons butter, onion, dry mustard, salt, pepper and hot pepper sauce in a bowl and mix well. Press into a 2$1/2$-cup mold. Chill, covered, for several hours. Unmold carefully onto a serving plate. Garnish with chopped hard-cooked egg.

Yield: 8 servings

Note: Pâté made with ground meat is a world-famous spread. Guests serve themselves with a knife or spoon and spread the pâté onto bread, toast, or crackers.

Warm Figs with Feta and Basil

2 tablespoons red wine vinegar
2 tablespoons honey
16 Black Mission figs
2 ounces feta cheese
16 large basil leaves

Combine the vinegar and honey in a saucepan. Bring to a simmer, stirring constantly. Keep warm.

Preheat a grill to medium-high or heat a grill pan over medium-high heat. Grill the figs for 4 minutes or until heated through, turning frequently. Remove to a platter. Cut open the figs using a small sharp knife.

Cut the cheese into 16 equal portions. Fold a basil leaf around each portion of cheese. Stuff each fig with cheese. Pour the vinegar mixture over the figs. Serve immediately.

Yield: 16 servings

Note: This hors d'oeuvre offers a wonderful combination of sweet, tangy, and herbal flavors and contrasting textures.

A FEW BEANS OR GRAINS OF RICE INSIDE A SALT SHAKER WILL KEEP IT FLOWING FREELY EVEN IN THE DAMPEST WEATHER.

Stuffed Mushrooms

24 medium mushrooms
1/4 green bell pepper, chopped
1/4 onion, chopped
1/2 tablespoon vegetable oil
1 1/2 to 2 pounds bulk pork sausage
1 egg
3 tablespoons bread crumbs
1/2 teaspoon salt
1/4 teaspoon pepper
Dash of poultry seasoning
1/2 teaspoon prepared mustard
Juice of 1 lemon
3 tablespoons grated Parmesan cheese

Rinse the mushrooms with cool water and pat dry. Remove and dice the mushroom stems, leaving the caps intact.

Sauté the mushroom stems, bell pepper and onion in the oil in a skillet until the onion is translucent; drain.

Combine the sausage, egg, bread crumbs, salt, pepper, poultry seasoning and mustard in a bowl and mix well. Add the sautéed mixture and mix well.

Stuff the mushroom caps with the sausage mixture. Arrange in a baking pan. Bake at 375 degrees for 30 to 35 minutes. Sprinkle with the lemon juice and Parmesan cheese. Serve immediately

Yield: 24 servings

Cheese Cookies

1 cup (4 ounces) shredded Cheddar cheese
1/2 cup (1 stick) butter, softened
1 cup Rice Krispies
1 cup flour
Cayenne pepper to taste

Combine the cheese, butter, cereal, flour and cayenne pepper in a bowl and mix well. Shape into 1¹/₂-inch balls. Arrange on ungreased baking sheets. Flatten with a fork. Bake at 325 degrees for 20 minutes. Remove to clean kitchen towels. Cool completely. Store in an airtight container.

Yield: 2 dozen cookies

Mints

3 ounces cream cheese, softened
2¹/₂ cups (or more) confectioners' sugar
1/8 teaspoon mint, clove or other flavoring
Food coloring

Beat the cream cheese in a large mixing bowl. Beat in 1 cup of the confectioners' sugar, flavoring and food coloring. Beat in enough of the remaining confectioners' sugar to make a stiff dough. Shape into small balls. Press into candy molds. Chill, covered, for a few minutes or until set. Remove carefully from the molds.

Yield: 50 servings

Note: It helps to roll the dough in granulated sugar
before pressing into candy molds.

Hot Mulled Cider

1/2 cup packed brown sugar
1 teaspoon allspice
1 teaspoon whole cloves
1/4 teaspoon salt
Dash of nutmeg
1 (3-inch) cinnamon stick
2 quarts apple cider
Orange wedges
Whole cloves

Combine the brown sugar, allspice, 1 teaspoon cloves, salt, nutmeg, cinnamon and apple cider in a saucepan. Bring to a boil over medium heat. Simmer, covered, for 20 minutes. Remove cloves and cinnamon. Stud the orange wedges with cloves. Serve the cider and clove-studded orange wedges in warm mugs.

Yield: 2 quarts

Trader's Punch

2 cups orange juice
2 cups lemon juice
1 cup grenadine syrup
1/2 cup light corn syrup
3 (28-ounce) bottles ginger ale, chilled

Combine the orange juice, lemon juice, grenadine syrup and corn syrup in a large container and mix well. Chill, covered, until serving time. Pour into a punch bowl. Add the ginger ale and mix well. Serve immediately.

Yield: 4 quarts

Golden Punch

6 cups water
3 cups sugar
1 (46-ounce) can pineapple juice
8 bananas
1 (12-ounce) can frozen lemonade concentrate, thawed
1 (16-ounce) can frozen orange juice concentrate, thawed
2 (3-liter) bottles ginger ale

Combine the water and sugar in a saucepan. Bring to a boil, stirring constantly. Let the sugar syrup stand to cool.

Combine half the pineapple juice and 4 bananas in a blender. Process until well blended. Pour into a large container. Repeat the procedure with the remaining pineapple juice and bananas. Add the sugar syrup, lemonade concentrate and orange juice concentrate and mix well. Divide equal portions of the mixture among 4 containers. Freeze, covered, until serving time. Combine 2 portions of the frozen mixture and 1 bottle ginger ale in a large container and mix well. Pour into a punch bowl. Repeat the procedure with the remaining frozen mixture and ginger ale.

Yield: 25 to 40 servings

WHEN ONE DOOR OF HAPPINESS CLOSES, ANOTHER OPENS; BUT

OFTEN WE LOOK SO LONG AT THE CLOSED DOOR THAT WE DO NOT

SEE THE ONE THAT HAS BEEN OPENED FOR US.

—Helen Keller

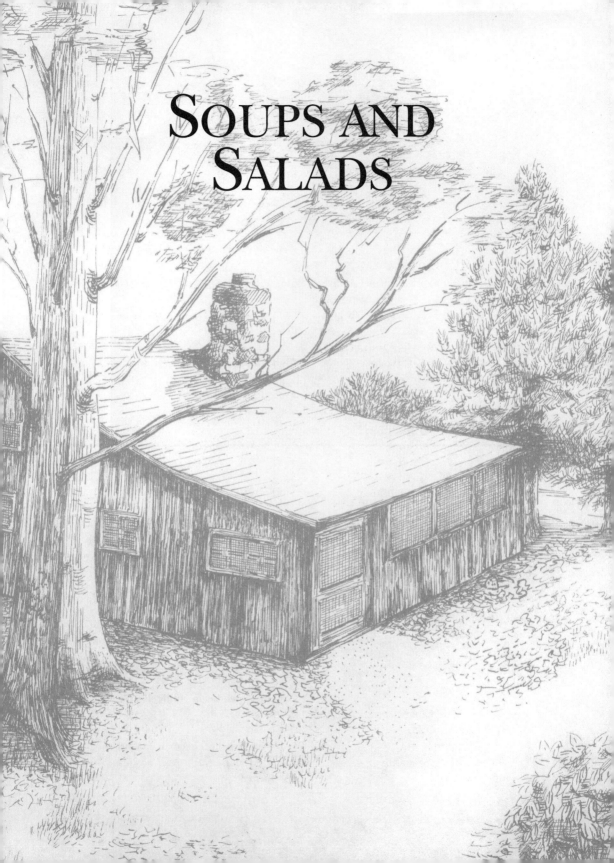

SOUPS AND SALADS

Salad Secrets

Chill ingredients before mixing—except for molded salads.

Provide tartness in the body of the salad or dressing.

Use salad greens other than lettuce sometimes. Have you tried chicory, endive, escarole, kale, spinach, romaine, dandelion greens, watercress, and Chinese cabbage?

Sprinkle orange, lemon, lime, or pineapple juice on fruits that may turn dark—apples, peaches, and bananas, for instance.

For tossed green salads, tear greens in fairly large pieces or cut with scissors. Larger pieces give more body to the salad.

Prevent wilting and sogginess by drying greens used in salads, draining canned foods well before adding to the salad, and using just enough salad dressing to moisten. For raw vegetable salads, add dressing at the last minute.

Fruit Combinations:

Sliced pineapple, apricot halves, sweet red cherries

Watermelon balls, peach slices, orange slices

Grapefruit sections, banana slices, berries, or cherries

Peach slices, pear slices, halves of red plums

Pineapple wedges, banana slices, strawberries

Cooked dried fruit, white cherries, red raspberries

Fruit and Vegetable Combinations:

Shredded carrots, diced apples, raisins

Sliced or ground cranberries, diced celery, diced apples, orange sections

Thin cucumber slices, pineapple cubes

Avocado slices, grapefruit sections, tomato slices

Shredded cabbage, orange sections, crushed pineapple

Vegetable Combinations:

Grated carrots, diced celery, cucumber slices

Spinach, endive, or lettuce with tomato wedges

Sliced cauliflower florets, chopped green bell pepper, celery, pimento

Shredded cabbage, cucumber cubes, slivers of celery

Cubed cooked beets, thinly sliced celery, sweet onions

Cooked whole kernel corn, cooked shredded snap beans, sweet pickles, onion rings

Sauerbraten Supreme Soup

1 (1-pound) boneless round steak ($^3/_4$ inch)
$^1/_4$ teaspoon ground cloves
1 tablespoon margarine
1 envelope onion soup mix
3 cups water
4 ounces noodles
1 teaspoon wine vinegar
$^1/_2$ cup crushed gingersnaps
1 package frozen green beans
1 medium bay leaf
Sour cream (optional)

Freeze the steak for 1 hour to make cutting easier. Cut into very thin strips. Sauté the steak and cloves in the margarine in a saucepan until the steak is browned. Remove to a plate.

Combine the soup mix and 3 cups water in a large saucepan. Cook using the package directions. Cook the noodles using the package directions; drain.

Add the steak, noodles, vinegar, gingersnaps, green beans and bay leaf to the onion soup and mix well. Simmer for 20 minutes, stirring occasionally and adding additional water if needed. Remove the bay leaf. Ladle into soup bowls. Top each serving with a dollop of sour cream.

Yield: 8 servings

Note: This is for anyone whose mother made sauerbraten
from scratch. This soup cannot replace it, but it is quick and the
taste is supreme. It is a good winter soup.

Special Three-Bean Chili

2¹/₂ pounds ground chuck
¹/₂ cup chopped onion
¹/₂ cup chopped green bell pepper
1 tablespoon apple cider vinegar
2 tablespoons brown sugar
1 teaspoon prepared or Dijon mustard
1 (15-ounce) can butter beans
1 (15-ounce) can kidney beans
1 can Bush's Best Bold & Spicy Baked Beans
1 can Bush's Best Onion Baked Beans
1 can Hunt's Chili Tomato Sauce, or
1 (6-ounce) can tomato paste and 1 can water

Brown the ground chuck with the onion and bell pepper in a skillet, stirring until crumbly; drain. Add the vinegar, brown sugar and mustard and mix well.

Combine the butter beans, kidney beans, baked beans and ground chuck in a slow cooker and mix well. Add the tomato sauce and mix well.

Cook on High until the mixture is heated through. Cook on Low for 8 to 10 hours. You may cook the chili in a saucepan over low heat for 30 minutes. Ladle into soup bowls. Serve with corn bread.

Yield: 8 to 10 servings

Note: You may add a small amount of chili powder if desired.

Autumn Soup

1 pound Polish kielbasa, chopped
1 large white onion, chopped
1 tablespoon corn oil
1 small head cabbage
4 large carrots, chopped
6 medium potatoes, chopped
2 (28-ounce) cans chunky garden-style spaghetti sauce

Cook the sausage and onion in the corn oil in a large saucepan over medium-high heat until the sausage is browned, stirring frequently.

Cut the cabbage into small wedges. Add the cabbage, carrots and potatoes to the sausage mixture and mix well. Stir in the spaghetti sauce. Cook over medium-low heat for 45 minutes or until the vegetables are tender, stirring occasionally and adding water if needed. Ladle into soup bowls and serve.

Yield: 6 servings

NEVER ASK OF THOSE WHO REPORT TO YOU THE PERFORMANCE

OF A TASK YOU WOULD NOT BE WILLING TO DO YOURSELF.

—*Johnetta B. Cole*

Miso Soup

1 (3-inch) strip wakame
2¹/2 cups water
¹/2 cup sliced carrot
¹/2 cup sliced kale or watercress
1 green onion, finely sliced
1 tablespoon barley miso (2-year, unpasteurized variety)

Cut the wakame into small pieces using scissors, or soak the wakame and cut with a knife.

Bring the water to a boil in a large saucepan. Add the wakame and carrot. Simmer for 15 minutes. Add the kale and mix well.

Cook for 5 minutes. Stir in the green onion. Simmer for 1 to 2 minutes. Turn off the heat.

Press the miso through a sieve into the soup using a spoon. Stir until the miso is dissolved. Ladle into soup bowls.

Yield: 4 servings

Note: You may substitute juicier vegetables, such as Chinese cabbage, fresh corn, radishes, green beans, or crookneck squash. You may try a lighter miso, such as low-sodium chick-pea miso.

Pumpkin Soup

1/4 cup (1/2 stick) butter
1 garlic clove, minced
1 onion, chopped
1 leek, chopped
1 apple, peeled and chopped
1 tablespoon curry powder
2 cups chopped fresh pumpkin
4 cups chicken broth
1 cup whipping cream
Salt and pepper to taste

Melt the butter in a saucepan. Add the garlic, onion, leek and apple. Sauté until the onion and apple are tender. Stir in the curry powder. Cook for 1 minute, stirring constantly.

Add the pumpkin and broth and mix well. Bring to a boil, stirring occasionally. Reduce the heat. Simmer until the vegetables are tender.

Pour the mixture into a blender or food processor. Process until puréed. Return to the saucepan. Stir in the whipping cream. Season with salt and pepper. Ladle into soup bowls.

Yield: 6 to 8 servings

NEVER TASTE FOOD WITH YOUR COOKING SPOON

BECAUSE BACTERIA WILL GET IN AND SPOIL

THE WHOLE POT.

Cream of Wild Rice Soup

1 large onion, chopped
¹/2 green bell pepper, chopped
1¹/2 ribs celery, chopped
2 large mushrooms, chopped, or
1 small can sliced mushrooms, drained
¹/2 cup (1 stick) butter
1 cup flour
8 cups chicken broth, heated
2 cups cooked wild rice
Salt and pepper to taste
1 cup light cream or half-and-half

Sauté the onion, bell pepper, celery and mushrooms in the butter in a skillet for 3 minutes or just until the vegetables are tender. Sprinkle with the flour.

Cook until the flour is incorporated, stirring constantly. Add the broth gradually, stirring constantly. Stir in the rice. Season with salt and pepper.

Cook until heated through. Stir in the cream. Cook over low heat until heated through; do not boil. Ladle into soup bowls and serve.

Yield: 12 servings

Easy Mexican Vegetable Soup

1 can Bush's Best Chili Hot Beans
1 can tomatoes
1 can whole kernel corn
3 cans water
4 green onions, chopped
$1/2$ green bell pepper, chopped
6 beef bouillon cubes
1 envelope taco seasoning mix
1 teaspoon honey
$1/2$ cup uncooked rice
Shredded sharp Cheddar cheese
Sour cream

Combine the beans, tomatoes, corn and water in a stockpot and mix well. Bring to a boil. Add the green onions, bell pepper, bouillon cubes, taco seasoning mix, honey and rice and mix well. Simmer for 1 hour, stirring occasionally. Ladle into soup bowls. Top each serving with Cheddar cheese and a dollop of sour cream. Serve with corn chips or tortilla chips.

Yield: 8 to 10 servings

Note: This would be an excellent camp meal.

THAT OLD LAW ABOUT "AN EYE FOR AN EYE"

LEAVES EVERYBODY BLIND.

—Dr. Martin Luther King, Jr.

Fresh Green Bean, Corn and Tomato Salad

6 ounces green beans
3 ears of white corn
1 tablespoon salt
$1/2$ cup white wine vinegar
6 tablespoons vegetable oil
5 tablespoons sugar
Pepper to taste
3 large tomatoes, chopped
$1/2$ red onion, chopped
$1/2$ cup chopped fresh parsley

Cut the green beans into 1-inch pieces. Cut the kernels from the corn.

Combine the green beans, salt and enough water to cover in a large skillet. Bring to a boil. Boil for 4 to 6 minutes. Add the corn. Cook for 3 to 5 minutes or until the vegetables are tender-crisp; drain. Rinse with cool water; drain well.

Combine the vinegar, oil and sugar in a large bowl and mix well using a whisk. Season with salt and pepper. Add the green beans, corn, tomatoes, onion and parsley and toss to mix well. Chill, covered, for 2 to 10 hours.

Yield: 4 to 8 servings

Note: You may use frozen vegetables. You may substitute asparagus, cucumber, or peas for the green beans or cilantro for the parsley.

Southwest Bean Salad

2 cups drained canned pinto beans
2 cups drained canned whole kernel corn
2 ribs celery, cut into $1/4$-inch pieces
1 large carrot, sliced or julienned
1 tablespoon coriander seeds, ground
$1/4$ cup green olives, chopped
$1/4$ cup olive oil
$1/4$ cup lemon or lime juice
1 teaspoon cumin
2 teaspoons mild chili powder
1 teaspoon salt
1 small jalapeño chile, chopped
1 garlic clove, minced

Combine the beans, corn, celery, carrot, coriander seeds and olives in a bowl and mix well.

Combine the olive oil, lemon juice, cumin, chili powder, salt, jalapeño chile and garlic in a jar with a tight-fitting lid and shake to mix well.

Pour the olive oil mixture over the bean mixture and toss to mix well. Adjust the seasonings and serve.

Yield: 4 to 6 servings

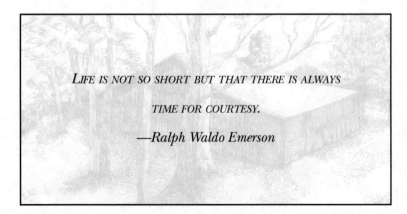

LIFE IS NOT SO SHORT BUT THAT THERE IS ALWAYS

TIME FOR COURTESY.

—Ralph Waldo Emerson

Imitation Greek Salad

3 cups chopped cooked lamb
2 medium cucumbers, peeled and sliced
2 medium tomatoes, chopped
1/2 cup chopped black olives
1/2 cup wine vinegar
1/2 cup chopped almonds
1 tablespoon lemon juice
1 teaspoon salt
1/2 teaspoon pepper

Combine the lamb, cucumbers, tomatoes, black olives, vinegar, almonds, lemon juice, salt and pepper in a bowl and mix well. Chill, covered, until serving time. You may serve this salad over lettuce or heat through and serve over rice and sprinkle with shredded cheese.

Yield: 4 servings

Note: You may add anchovies.

Shrimp Salad

3 small cans cocktail shrimp, drained
1 medium head lettuce, chopped
2 ribs celery, chopped
2 medium tomatoes, chopped
Salt and pepper to taste
2 tablespoons Catalina or French salad dressing
5 heaping tablespoons mayonnaise

Combine the shrimp, lettuce, celery, tomatoes, salt and pepper in a bowl and mix well. Combine the salad dressing and mayonnaise in a bowl and mix well. Add to the shrimp mixture and toss lightly to mix.

Yield: 6 to 8 servings

Tabouli

³/4 cup bulgur
1¹/2 cups snipped fresh parsley
3 tomatoes, chopped
¹/3 cup chopped green onions
Chopped black olives to taste (optional)
2 tablespoons chopped fresh mint (optional)
¹/4 cup olive oil
¹/4 cup lemon juice
1 teaspoon salt
¹/4 teaspoon freshly ground pepper

Combine the bulgur and enough hot water to cover in a bowl. Let stand for 30 minutes; drain. Combine the bulgur, parsley, tomatoes, green onions, black olives, mint, olive oil, lemon juice, salt and pepper in a bowl and mix well. Chill, covered, until serving time.

Yield: 4 to 6 servings

THERE ARE A FEW POSSESSIONS WHICH

ONCE GONE ARE IMPOSSIBLE TO RECAPTURE.

YOUR INTEGRITY IS ONE OF THEM.

—*Johnetta B. Cole*

Copper Penny Salad

1 can tomato soup
1 tablespoon Worcestershire sauce
1/2 cup vinegar
1/2 cup vegetable oil
1 cup sugar
2 pounds carrots, parboiled, drained and sliced, or
2 cans sliced carrots, drained
1 green bell pepper, chopped
1 red onion, sliced
Chopped celery to taste

Combine the soup, Worcestershire sauce, vinegar, oil and sugar in a saucepan. Bring to a boil, stirring frequently. Remove from the heat. Combine the carrots, bell pepper, onion and celery in a bowl and mix well. Add the tomato soup mixture and mix well. Chill, covered, for 24 hours.

Yield: 6 to 8 servings

Note: This is the only way I can get the adult males in my family to eat carrots.

ALWAYS BRUISE YOUR GREENS A LITTLE WHEN WASHING

THEM. IT MAKES FOR BETTER TASTE.

Layered Lettuce Salad

1 package frozen peas
1 head lettuce, cut into bite-size pieces
1 cup chopped celery
4 hard-cooked eggs, chopped
1/2 cup chopped green bell pepper
1 sweet onion, chopped
8 slices bacon, crisp-cooked and crumbled
2 cups mayonnaise
1/2 cup Miracle Whip Salad Dressing
2 tablespoons sugar
4 ounces (1 cup) shredded Cheddar cheese

Cook the peas using the package directions; drain. Layer the lettuce, celery, eggs, peas, bell pepper, onion and bacon in a 9×12-inch dish. Combine the mayonnaise, salad dressing and sugar in a bowl and mix well. Spread over the layers. Sprinkle with the cheese. Chill, covered, for 8 to 12 hours. Garnish with chopped fresh parsley and additional crumbled crisp-cooked bacon if desired.

Yield: 6 to 8 servings

Note: This dish is great for family gatherings, picnics, and church socials.

Crunchy Coleslaw

1 package chicken-flavor ramen noodles, broken into small pieces
1 (16-ounce) package coleslaw mix
1 (3-ounce) package slivered almonds, toasted
1/2 cup vegetable oil
1/4 cup sugar
2 tablespoons vinegar
Salt and pepper to taste

Reserve the seasoning packet from the ramen noodles. Combine the ramen noodles, coleslaw mix and almonds in a bowl and mix well. Combine the oil, sugar, vinegar, reserved seasoning, salt and pepper in a bowl and mix well. Pour over the ramen noodle mixture and mix well. Serve immediately.

Yield: 12 servings

I DON'T KNOW THE KEY TO SUCCESS, BUT THE KEY

TO FAILURE IS TRYING TO PLEASE EVERYBODY.

—Bill Cosby

MAIN DISHES

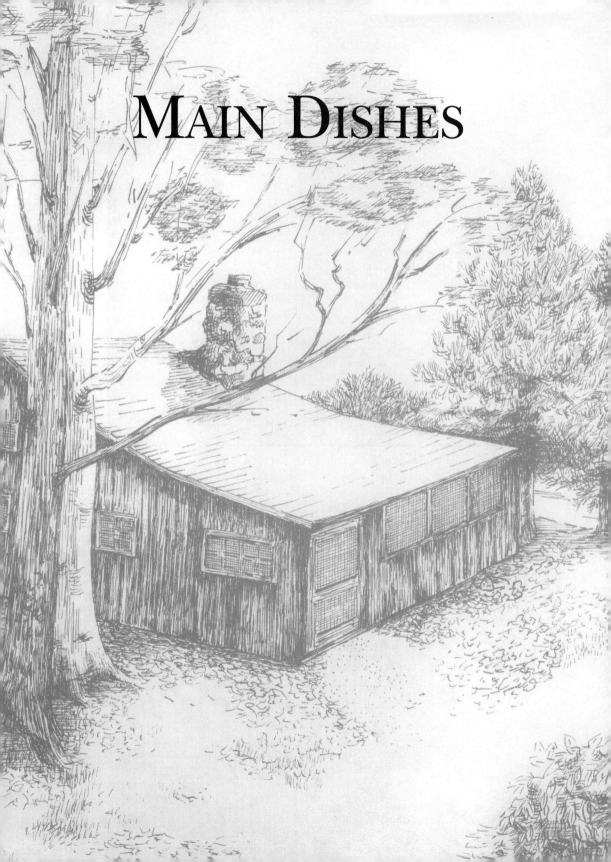

Kitchen Ideas

A leaf of lettuce dropped into the pot absorbs grease from the top of the soup. Remove the lettuce and throw it away as soon as it has served its purpose.

To prevent splashing when frying meat, sprinkle a little salt into the pan before putting the fat in.

Small amounts of leftover corn may be added to pancake batter for variety.

To make bread crumbs, use the fine cutter of the food grinder and tie a large paper bag over the spout to prevent flying crumbs.

When bread is baking, a small dish of water in the oven will help keep the crust from getting hard.

Rinse a pan in cold water before scalding milk to prevent sticking.

When you are creaming butter and sugar together, it is a good idea to rinse the bowl with boiling water first. They'll cream faster.

To melt chocolate, grease the pan in which it is to be melted.

Dip the spoon in hot water to measure shortening, butter, etc.—the fat will slip out more easily.

When you buy cellophane-wrapped cupcakes and notice that the cellophane is somewhat stuck to the frosting, hold the package under the cold-water tap for a moment before you unwrap it. The cellophane will come off cleanly.

When you are baking, you get better results if you remember to preheat your cookie sheet, muffin tins, or cake pans.

Chill cheese to grate it more easily.

The odor from baking or broiling salmon may be eliminated by squeezing lemon juice on both sides of each salmon steak or on the cut surface of the salmon and letting it stand in the refrigerator for one hour or longer before cooking.

Use the type of can opener that leaves a smooth edge and remove both ends from a flat can (the size can that tuna is usually packed in) and you have a perfect mold for poaching eggs.

Use the divider from an ice tray to cut biscuits in a hurry. Shape dough to conform to the size of the divider and cut. After baking, the biscuits will separate at the dividing lines.

Try using a thread instead of a knife when a cake is to be cut while it is hot.

Herbed Pot Roast

1 (3- to 3¹/2-pound) boneless beef rump roast or chuck roast
1 tablespoon vegetable oil
1 teaspoon salt
1 teaspoon marjoram
1 teaspoon thyme
¹/2 teaspoon oregano
¹/2 teaspoon garlic powder
¹/2 teaspoon pepper
1 (10-ounce) can beef broth
8 carrots, cut into thirds
8 medium potatoes, peeled and quartered
1 large onion, quartered
1 cup water

Brown the roast in the oil in a Dutch oven. Combine the salt, marjoram, thyme, oregano, garlic powder and pepper in a bowl and mix well. Sprinkle over the roast. Add the broth. Bring to a boil. Bake, covered, at 325 degrees for 2 hours, basting occasionally. Add the carrots, potatoes, onion and water. Bake, covered, for 1 hour or until the vegetables are tender. You may use the pan drippings to make gravy if desired.

Yield: 8 servings

> *WASTE YOUR MONEY AND YOU'RE ONLY OUT OF MONEY,*
>
> *BUT WASTE YOUR TIME AND YOU'VE LOST A PART OF YOUR LIFE.*
>
> —*Michael Leboeuf*

Beef Stew

2 (15-ounce) cans Veg-All Original Mixed Vegetables
2 (14-ounce) cans sliced potatoes
1 can corn
2 beef bouillon cubes
1 envelope onion soup mix
1 to 2 pounds beef stew meat
Water (optional)
Salt and pepper to taste

Combine the undrained mixed vegetables, potatoes and corn in a slow cooker and mix well. Add the bouillon cubes and soup mix and mix well. Stir in the beef. Add water if more liquid is needed. Cook on Low for 8 to 10 hours or until the beef is tender. You may cook on High for 3 to 4 hours. Season with salt and pepper. You may freeze any leftovers. Cook leftover stew in a saucepan until heated through.

Yield: 6 to 8 servings

IT IS FAR BETTER TO LEARN TO WALK FULLY IN YOUR OWN FOOTPRINTS THAN TO FORCE A FIT INTO SOMEONE ELSE'S.

—Johnetta B. Cole

Stuffed Peppers

1 pound ground beef or turkey
$^1/_2$ cup chopped onion
3 tablespoons prepared mustard
2 bags boil-in-bag rice, or 2 cups rice
3 medium to large green bell peppers
2 cans Campbell's Tomato Juice
6 slices longhorn cheese

Brown the ground beef with the onion and mustard in a skillet, stirring until the ground beef is crumbly; drain. Cook the rice using the package directions.

Cut the bell peppers into halves, discarding the seeds and fleshy membranes. Combine the bell peppers with enough water to cover in a saucepan. Bring to a boil. Boil for 20 minutes; drain.

Combine the ground beef mixture and rice in a bowl and mix well. Stuff the bell peppers with the mixture, filling to overflowing. Arrange in a 9×11-inch baking dish. Pour half the tomato juice gradually over the bell peppers to season the filling. Place a cheese slice on top of each bell pepper. Pour the remaining tomato juice over the cheese and around the bell peppers. Bake at 400 degrees for 20 to 25 minutes or until the cheese starts to brown.

Yield: 6 servings

Note: You may substitute spaghetti sauce for the tomato juice.

Cheese-Stuffed Meat Loaf

2 small onions, minced
Vegetable oil
2 pounds ground beef
2 eggs
1/2 cup seasoned bread crumbs
1 cup tomato juice
1 teaspoon oregano
1/2 teaspoon salt
Pepper to taste
8 thin slices boiled ham
8 ounces mozzarella cheese, shredded

Sauté the onions in a small amount of oil in a skillet until golden brown. Combine the onions, ground beef, eggs, bread crumbs, tomato juice, oregano, salt and pepper in a bowl and mix well. Place on a large piece of foil. Flatten into an 8×12-inch rectangle. Arrange the ham on top within 1 inch of the edge. Sprinkle with the cheese. Fold the meat mixture in half crosswise using the foil. Seal the edges of the meat mixture. Remove from the foil. Place in a 5×8-inch loaf pan, shaping into a loaf and pressing to fill the corners; the top should be rounded. Bake at 325 degrees for 60 to 75 minutes.

Yield: 4 to 6 servings

IF YOU HAVE OVERSALTED VEGETABLES OR SOUP, ADDING A

SLICE OF RAW POTATO WILL REMEDY THE SITUATION.

Onion Meat Loaf

2 pounds ground beef
1 envelope onion soup mix
1 egg
2/3 cup milk
3 tablespoons brown sugar
3 tablespoons ketchup
1 tablespoon prepared mustard

Combine the ground beef, soup mix and egg in a bowl and mix well. Shape into a loaf. Place in a loaf pan. Combine the milk, brown sugar, ketchup and mustard in a bowl and mix well. Spoon evenly over the meat loaf. Bake for 1 hour. Let stand for 10 minutes before serving.

Yield: 4 to 6 servings

Meatballs

1 pound ground beef
1 envelope Lipton Onion Soup Mix
2/3 cup (1 small can) evaporated milk
2 teaspoons Worcestershire sauce
2 cups ketchup
1 cup packed brown sugar
1 tablespoon Worcestershire sauce

Combine the ground beef, soup mix, evaporated milk and 2 teaspoons Worcestershire sauce in a bowl and mix well. Shape into balls using a meatballer. Arrange on a broiler pan sprayed with nonstick cooking spray. Bake at 350 degrees for 12 to 15 minutes or until browned. Combine the ketchup, brown sugar and 1 tablespoon Worcestershire sauce in a large saucepan. Cook over medium heat for 10 minutes, stirring frequently. Add the meatballs and stir gently to coat. Serve immediately.

Yield: 15 to 20 meatballs

Spaghetti Pie

8 ounces spaghetti
2 eggs, beaten
2/3 cup grated Parmesan cheese
2 tablespoons margarine, softened
2 cups cottage cheese, drained
2 eggs, beaten
1 pound ground beef or Italian sausage
1/2 cup chopped onion
1/2 cup chopped green bell pepper
2 cups spaghetti sauce
1 cup (4 ounces) shredded mozzarella cheese

Cook the spaghetti using the package directions; drain. Combine 2 eggs, Parmesan cheese and margarine in a large bowl and mix well. Add the hot spaghetti and mix well. Press onto the bottom and up the side of two 8-inch pie plates or two 8×8-inch baking dishes.

Combine the cottage cheese and 2 eggs in a bowl and mix well. Spread equal portions of the mixture evenly over the spaghetti mixture.

Brown the ground beef with the onion and bell pepper in a large skillet, stirring until the ground beef is crumbly; drain. Stir in the spaghetti sauce. Cook until heated through. Spread over the cottage cheese mixture. Bake at 350 degrees for 20 minutes. Sprinkle with the mozzarella cheese. Bake until the cheese is melted. Let stand for 5 minutes. Cut into wedges to serve.

Yield: 8 to 10 servings

String Pie

1 pound ground beef
1/2 cup chopped onion
1/4 cup chopped green bell pepper
2 cups spaghetti sauce
8 ounces spaghetti, cooked
1/3 cup grated Parmesan cheese
2 eggs, beaten
2 teaspoons butter, softened
1 cup cottage cheese
1/2 cup (2 ounces) shredded mozzarella cheese

Brown the ground beef with the onion and bell pepper in a large skillet, stirring until the ground beef is crumbly; drain. Stir in the spaghetti sauce.

Combine the spaghetti, Parmesan cheese, eggs and butter in a bowl and mix well. Press into the bottom of a 9×13-inch baking pan. Spread with the cottage cheese.

Spoon the ground beef mixture evenly over the cottage cheese. Sprinkle with the mozzarella cheese. Bake at 350 degrees for 20 minutes or until the mixture is heated through and the cheese is melted.

Yield: 6 to 8 servings

IF YOU TELL THE TRUTH, YOU DON'T HAVE

TO REMEMBER ANYTHING.

—Mark Twain

Italian Fondue

8 ounces ground beef
1/2 envelope spaghetti sauce mix
1 (15-ounce) can tomato sauce
12 ounces Cheddar cheese, shredded
4 ounces mozzarella cheese, shredded
1 tablespoon cornstarch
1/2 cup (about) water

Brown the ground beef in a large skillet, stirring until crumbly; drain. Stir in the spaghetti sauce mix and tomato sauce. Simmer for several minutes, stirring occasionally. Add the cheese gradually, stirring constantly. Cook over low heat until the cheese is melted, stirring constantly. Dissolve the cornstarch in a small amount of water in a cup. Add to the ground beef mixture and mix well. Stir in 1/2 cup water. Cook until heated through, stirring constantly. Serve with Italian bread cubes for dipping.

Yield: 6 servings

Meat and Main Dish

1 pound ground beef
1 medium onion, chopped
3 cups chopped celery
1 cup chopped green bell pepper
1/2 cup water
1 (10-ounce) can cream of mushroom soup
1 (4-ounce) can chow mein noodles

Brown the ground beef in a large skillet, stirring until crumbly; drain. Stir in the onion, celery, bell pepper and water. Cook until tender, stirring frequently. Stir in the soup. Cook until heated through. Stir in the noodles. Spoon into a 9×13-inch baking dish. Bake at 350 degrees for 30 minutes.

Yield: 4 servings

Abuelita's Mashed Potato Casserole

2 pounds lean ground beef or ground round
1/2 cup chopped green bell pepper
1/2 cup chopped onion
Garlic salt and pepper to taste
2 (10-ounce) cans tomato soup
2 (14-ounce) cans French-style green beans, drained
Mashed potatoes
Paprika to taste

Brown the ground beef with the bell pepper and onion in a skillet, stirring until the ground beef is crumbly; drain. Add garlic salt and pepper and mix well. Stir in the tomato soup, adding water if needed. Add the green beans and mix well. Simmer for 10 minutes. Spoon into a 9×13-inch baking dish. Top with mounds of mashed potatoes. Sprinkle the potatoes with paprika. Bake at 350 degrees for 30 minutes or until heated through.

Yield: 6 servings

BRUSH FRESH MEAT WITH OLIVE OIL BEFORE WRAPPING

FOR THE FREEZER. IT WILL KEEP THE MEAT MOIST.

Lance's Far East Marinade for Pork Loin

1 (12-ounce) bottle Kikkoman Teriyaki Marinade
1 small can crushed pineapple
6 ounces soy sauce
3 tablespoons brown sugar
4 garlic cloves, crushed
6 ounces water or pineapple juice
Pork loin

Combine the teriyaki marinade, pineapple, soy sauce, brown sugar, garlic and water in a bowl and mix well. Pour the marinade into a sealable plastic bag. Add pork loin. Chill for 8 to 10 hours. Grill to 150 degrees on a meat thermometer, turning and basting frequently with the marinade.

Yield: 4 cups

THE BEST EXECUTIVE IS THE ONE WHO HAS SENSE ENOUGH TO PICK GOOD MEN TO DO WHAT HE WANTS DONE, AND SELF-RESTRAINT ENOUGH TO KEEP FROM MEDDLING WITH THEM WHILE THEY DO IT.

—Theodore Roosevelt

Cheese and Ham Strata

8 slices white bread, crusts trimmed
Butter
4 slices Cheddar or American cheese
4 slices deli ham
4 eggs
2¹/2 cups milk
¹/2 teaspoon salt
1 teaspoon Worcestershire sauce
¹/8 teaspoon paprika
2 tablespoons prepared mustard
1 tablespoon minced onion (optional)

Spread one side of the bread slices with butter. Arrange half the bread butter side down in an 8×8-inch baking dish. Layer with the cheese and ham. Arrange the remaining bread butter side up on top of the ham.

Combine the eggs, milk, salt, Worcestershire sauce, paprika, mustard and onion in a bowl and mix well. Pour over the layers in the baking dish. Chill, covered, for 8 to 10 hours.

Bake at 350 degrees for 1 hour or until a knife inserted in the center comes out clean and the top is golden brown.

For breakfast, serve with a fresh fruit salad, melon slices or other fresh fruit. For lunch or dinner, serve with a tossed green salad with salad dressing of choice and grilled tomato halves sprinkled with salt, pepper, a pinch of crumbled basil and oregano, then dotted with butter and broiled until heated through. You may double the recipe and bake in a 9×12-inch baking dish.

Yield: 4 servings

Breakfast Pizza

1 pound bulk pork sausage
1 (8-count) package crescent rolls
1 cup frozen hash brown potatoes, thawed
1 cup (4 ounces) shredded sharp cheese
5 eggs
1 cup milk
Salt and pepper to taste
2 tablespoons grated Parmesan cheese

Brown the sausage in a skillet, stirring until crumbly; drain. Press the dough over the bottom of a pizza pan. Layer with the sausage, potatoes and sharp cheese. Beat the eggs, milk, salt and pepper in a bowl. Pour over the layers. Sprinkle with the Parmesan cheese. Bake at 375 degrees for 25 to 30 minutes.

Yield: 4 to 6 servings

Breakfast Casserole

8 slices white bread, cubed
1¹/₂ pounds bulk pork sausage, browned
2 cups (8 ounces) shredded sharp cheese
4 eggs
³/₄ teaspoon dry mustard
2¹/₂ cups milk
1 (10-ounce) can cream of mushroom soup
¹/₂ cup milk

Spread the bread cubes in the bottom of an 8×12-inch baking dish. Layer the sausage and cheese over the bread. Beat the eggs, dry mustard and 2¹/₂ cups milk in a bowl. Pour over the layers. Chill, covered, for 8 to 10 hours. Combine the soup and ¹/₂ cup milk in a bowl and mix well. Pour over the egg mixture. Bake at 300 degrees for 1¹/₂ hours.

Yield: 6 servings

Brunch Casserole

1 pound bulk pork sausage
4¹/2 cups dry bread cubes
2 cups (8 ounces) shredded sharp Cheddar cheese
10 eggs, lightly beaten
4 cups milk
1 teaspoon dry mustard
1 teaspoon salt
¹/4 teaspoon onion powder
Freshly ground pepper to taste
¹/2 cup sliced mushrooms (optional)

Brown the sausage in a skillet, stirring until crumbly; drain.

Spread the bread cubes in the bottom of a buttered 9×13-inch baking dish. Sprinkle with the cheese. Combine the eggs, milk, dry mustard, salt, onion powder and pepper in a bowl and mix well. Pour evenly over the cheese. Sprinkle with the sausage and mushrooms. Chill, covered, for 8 to 10 hours. Bake, uncovered, at 325 degrees for 1 hour, tenting with foil if top begins to browns too quickly.

Yield: 6 servings

SAUSAGE PATTIES ROLLED IN FLOUR WILL NOT

CRACK OPEN DURING FRYING.

Home-Style Good Morning Casserole

4 slices bread, crusts trimmed
6 eggs
1½ cups skim or low-fat milk
4 slices turkey bacon, cooked and crumbled
¼ cup shredded Cheddar cheese
¼ cup shredded Swiss cheese
⅓ cup sliced mushrooms
¼ teaspoon seasoned salt (optional)
½ cup frozen hash brown potatoes, thawed

Arrange the bread in the bottom of a 9×9-inch baking dish, overlapping slices if necessary. Combine the eggs, milk, bacon, half the Cheddar cheese, half the Swiss cheese, mushrooms and seasoned salt in a bowl and mix well. Pour evenly over the bread. Layer with the potatoes and remaining cheese. Chill, covered, for 8 to 10 hours. Bake, uncovered, at 350 degrees for 40 to 45 minutes or until a knife inserted in the center comes out clean and the top is lightly browned. You may add chopped green bell pepper, onion, tomatoes or cooked ham to the egg mixture.

Yield: 4 servings

Note: Wonderful for Christmas morning!

DO NOT FOLLOW WHERE THE PATH MAY LEAD. GO INSTEAD

WHERE THERE IS NO PATH AND LEAVE A TRAIL.

—Muriel Strode

Creamy Baked Chicken Breasts

4 whole boneless skinless chicken breasts, cut into halves
8 (4×4-inch) slices Swiss cheese
1 (10-ounce) can cream of chicken soup
1/2 cup milk or water
1/4 cup dry white wine
1 cup herb-seasoned stuffing mix
1/4 cup (1/2 stick) butter or margarine, melted

Arrange the chicken in a single layer in a greased baking dish. Place a cheese slice on top of each piece of chicken. Combine the soup, milk and wine in a bowl and mix well. Spoon evenly over the chicken. Sprinkle with the stuffing mix. Drizzle with the butter. Bake at 350 degrees for 1 hour or until the chicken is cooked through.

Yield: 8 servings

Oven-Baked Chicken

1/2 cup fat-free sour cream
1 tablespoon lemon juice
1 teaspoon each Worcestershire sauce and salt
1/2 teaspoon paprika
Dash of pepper
1 garlic clove, pressed
1 cup Town House Crackers, coarsely crumbled
6 boneless skinless chicken breasts
3 tablespoons butter, melted

Mix the first 7 ingredients in a bowl. Coat the chicken with the sour cream mixture. Roll in the cracker crumbs. Arrange on a foil-lined baking sheet. Drizzle with the butter. Bake at 350 degrees for 45 to 60 minutes or until cooked through and lightly browned.

Yield: 6 servings

Pecan Mustard Chicken

3/4 cup (1 1/2 sticks) butter or margarine
1/4 cup Champagne mustard
4 boneless skinless chicken breasts
3/4 cup chopped pecans
2 cups sour cream
3 tablespoons Champagne mustard

Combine the butter and 1/4 cup Champagne mustard in a saucepan. Cook until the butter is melted, stirring constantly. Dip the chicken in the butter mixture, reserving the remaining butter mixture. Coat with the pecans. Arrange in a baking dish. Pour the reserved butter mixture over the chicken. Bake, loosely covered with foil, at 400 degrees for 30 minutes. Bake, uncovered, for 10 to 15 minutes or until browned but not dry. Remove the chicken to a plate, reserving the pan drippings. Combine the sour cream, 3 tablespoons Champagne mustard and reserved pan drippings in a bowl and whisk to mix well. Spoon 1/4 cup of the mixture onto each of 4 individual serving plates. Top with the chicken. Serve with baked potatoes and the remaining sour cream mixture.

Yield: 4 servings

Note: If Champagne mustard is unavailable, another sweet mustard or Dijon mustard may be substituted.

Rice Krispies Chicken

2 cups crushed Rice Krispies
1 teaspoon salt
1/4 teaspoon pepper
1/4 teaspoon garlic powder
1 teaspoon paprika
1 (2 1/2-pound) chicken, cut up and skinned, or 4 to 6 skinless chicken pieces
1/2 cup (1 stick) butter or margarine, melted

Combine the cereal, salt, pepper, garlic powder and paprika in a bowl and mix well. Dip the chicken in the butter. Coat with the cereal mixture. Arrange in a baking pan. Bake, loosely covered with foil, at 350 degrees for 1 hour or until the chicken is cooked through.

Yield: 4 to 6 servings

A FEW DROPS OF LEMON JUICE ADDED TO SIMMERING RICE

WILL KEEP THE GRAINS FROM STICKING.

Chicken and Broccoli over Rice

1 small onion, chopped
1/2 cup (1 stick) butter or margarine
1 (10-ounce) can cream of chicken soup
1 cup sour cream
1 cup chicken broth
4 boneless skinless chicken breasts
2 cups chopped broccoli
Hot cooked rice or noodles

Combine the onion and butter in a 9×13-inch baking dish. Bake at 350 degrees until the onion begins to brown. Add the soup, sour cream and broth and mix well. Add the chicken, turning to coat. Add the broccoli. Bake for 1 hour. Serve over rice. You may chop the chicken before adding to the soup mixture.

Yield: 4 servings

Company Chicken Casserole

1 (10-ounce) can cream of mushroom soup
1 (10-ounce) can cream of chicken or celery soup
2 cups milk
1 cup uncooked rice
1 chicken, cut up, or 6 chicken pieces
1 envelope onion soup mix

Combine the soup and milk in a bowl and mix well. Stir in the rice. Pour into a baking dish or pan. Arrange the chicken on top. Sprinkle with the soup mix. Bake, covered with foil, at 350 degrees for 2 hours. Bake, uncovered, for 30 minutes.

Yield: 6 servings

Chicken Casserole

1 package chipped beef
8 boneless skinless chicken breasts
8 slices bacon
1 (10-ounce) can cream of mushroom soup
1 cup sour cream
1 cup water

Chop the beef coarsely. Spread in the bottom of a greased baking dish. Wrap each chicken breast with a slice of bacon. Arrange the chicken on top of the beef. Combine the soup, sour cream and water in a bowl and mix well. Pour evenly over the chicken. Bake at 275 degrees for 3 hours.

Yield: 8 servings

Note: Partially cooking the bacon before wrapping the chicken will reduce the amount of bacon fat in the sauce.

THE BEAUTY OF GENUINE BROTHERHOOD AND PEACE IS

MORE PRECIOUS THAN DIAMONDS OR SILVER OR GOLD.

—Dr. Martin Luther King, Jr.

Nancy's Turkey Pie

1/2 cup (1 stick) butter or margarine, softened
1 cup sour cream
1 egg
1 cup flour
1 teaspoon baking powder
1 teaspoon salt
1/3 cup sliced carrots
1/3 cup peas
1/3 cup chopped onion
1/3 cup chopped celery
2 cups chopped cooked turkey or chicken
1 (10-ounce) can cream of chicken soup
1/2 cup (2 ounces) shredded Cheddar cheese

Combine the butter, sour cream, egg, flour, baking powder and salt in a bowl and mix well. Press onto the bottom and up the side of a pie plate. Combine the carrots, peas, onion, celery, turkey and soup in a bowl and mix well. Spoon into the prepared pie plate. Sprinkle with the cheese. Bake at 375 degrees for 1 hour. Let stand for 15 minutes before serving.

Yield: 8 servings

Maryland Crab Cakes

3 slices dry white bread, crusts trimmed
1 egg, beaten
1 tablespoon mayonnaise
1 tablespoon Dijon mustard
1 teaspoon (or more) Chesapeake seasoning
1 tablespoon snipped fresh parsley (optional)
1 pound jumbo lump or back-fin crab meat, flaked
Vegetable oil for frying

Tear the bread into small pieces. Combine the bread and egg in a bowl and mix well. Add the mayonnaise, Dijon mustard, Chesapeake seasoning and parsley and mix well. Place the crab meat in a large bowl. Add the egg mixture and toss gently, keeping the crab meat in lumps. Shape into eight 3-inch patties. Arrange on a tray. Chill, covered with waxed paper, for 1 hour. Heat a small amount of oil in a heavy skillet. Fry the crab cakes in the hot oil for 8 minutes or until cooked through, turning once. Remove to paper towels using a slotted spatula.

Yield: 8 servings

To the expression "put your money where your mouth is," we would do well to add the request that each of us put some money where our hearts are—give to the causes you care about.

—Johnetta B. Cole

Crab Meat Quiche

1 (1-crust) pie pastry
1 egg white
1 cup (4 ounces) shredded Swiss cheese
2 cups half-and-half
2 eggs, beaten
1 teaspoon salt
1/8 teaspoon cayenne pepper (optional)
1 cup flaked crab meat

Fit the pastry into a 9-inch pie plate. Brush with the egg white. Place in the freezer while preparing the filling. Combine the cheese, half-and-half, eggs, salt and cayenne pepper in a bowl and mix well. Stir in the crab meat. Pour into the chilled pie shell. Bake at 425 degrees for 30 minutes or until a knife inserted in the center comes out clean. May be prepared ahead and frozen. Prepare as directed and bake for 30 minutes; cool. Wrap securely and freeze. Unwrap the quiche and place in a cold oven. Set oven temperature at 325 degrees. Bake for 20 to 25 minutes.

Yield: 6 servings

Grilled Salmon Teriyaki

3 tablespoons soy sauce
3 tablespoons dry wine
1 tablespoon sugar
1 teaspoon finely chopped fresh gingerroot
1 garlic clove, crushed or minced
4 (5- to 6-ounce) 1-inch salmon steaks
1 tablespoon canola oil

Combine the soy sauce, wine, sugar, gingerroot and garlic in a bowl and mix well. Brush the salmon with the canola oil. Arrange on an oiled grill rack. Grill 4 to 6 inches from heat for 5 to 6 minutes, brushing frequently with the soy sauce mixture. Turn over the salmon carefully using a large spatula. Brush with the soy sauce mixture. Grill for 5 to 6 minutes or until the center of the salmon is opaque and begins to flake. Remove salmon carefully to a plate. Serve immediately.

Yield: 4 servings

REMOVE A CAKE FROM A PAN BY PLACING A COLD TOWEL ON THE BOTTOM OF THE PAN. IT COMES OUT SMOOTH EVERY TIME.

Family Casserole

16 ounces rotini
1¹/2 pounds mild Cheddar cheese, shredded
1 (16-ounce) can tomatoes
6 ounces cleaned salmon, drained, or
12 ounces uncleaned salmon, drained and cleaned

Cook the rotini in a large saucepan using the package directions; drain. Return to the saucepan. Add the cheese and mix well; cover. Let stand until the cheese is melted. Drain the tomatoes, reserving the juice. Chop the tomatoes. Add the salmon, tomatoes and reserved juice to the rotini mixture and mix well. Spoon into a serving dish. Serve immediately.

Yield: 7 servings

Note: This is a one-pot dish that is much better served the next day.

Bean Sandwiches from Grandma Lange

4 slices bread
1 can baked beans
8 ounces (2 cups) shredded longhorn or Cheddar cheese
8 slices bacon, partially cooked

Toast the bread. Arrange on a baking sheet. Spread the beans over the bread. Sprinkle with the cheese. Arrange 2 bacon slices in an X pattern on top of each sandwich. Broil until the bacon is browned. Serve with a salad or canned peaches.

Yield: 4 servings

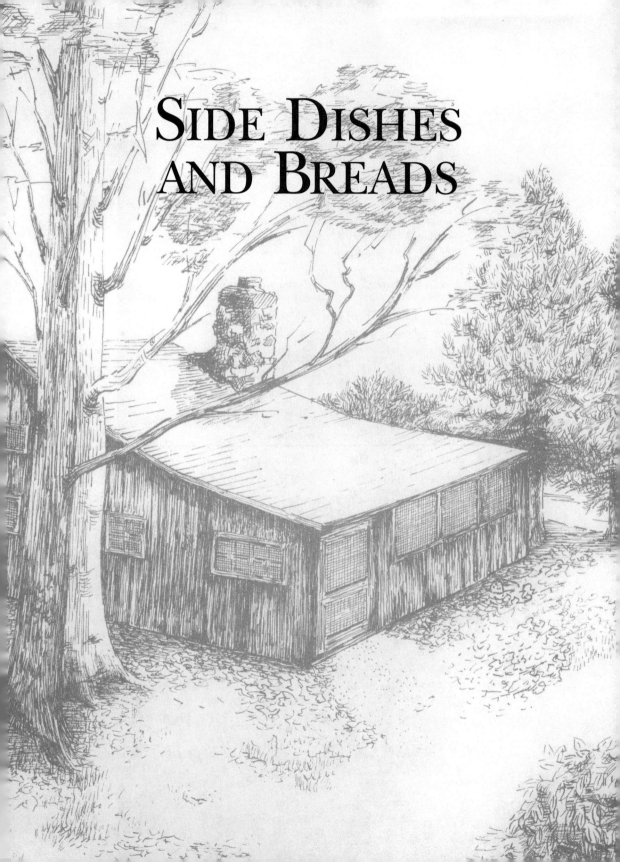

SIDE DISHES
AND BREADS

Tidbits

A pie crust will be more easily made and better if all of the ingredients are cool.

The bottom pastry of a pie should be placed in the pan so that it covers the surface smoothly. And be sure no air lurks beneath the surface, because it will push the crust out of shape while baking.

In making custard-type pies, bake the pie at a high temperature for about 10 minutes to prevent a soggy crust. Then finish baking at a low temperature.

Fill cake pans about two-thirds full and spread batter well into the corners and to the sides, leaving a slight hollow in the center.

A cake is done when it shrinks slightly from the sides of the pan or if it springs back when touched lightly with a finger.

After a cake is removed from the oven, it should be placed on a rack for about five minutes. Then the sides should be loosened and the cake turned out on the rack to finish cooling.

Cakes should not be frosted until thoroughly cooled.

Kneading the dough for 30 seconds after mixing improves the texture of baking powder biscuits.

Freeze leftover chicken or beef stock in ice trays. Then remove the frozen cubes, place in plastic bags, and store in the freezer for future use.

For tender corn on the cob, add $1/2$ cup milk and 1 teaspoon sugar to the boiling water before dropping in the corn.

Put cinnamon on the corner of the pot when cooking anything with a cabbage flavor to remove the smell.

When putting batter into a pan, spoon out the middle section and fill in each end. This will make the cake level.

When baking a cake, make sure all ingredients are at room temperature before mixing.

Before baking, cut a triangle in the batter with a knife to remove air bubbles.

If your cake calls for nuts, heat them first in the oven, then dust with flour before adding to the batter. Then they will not settle to the bottom of the pan.

Cream will whip faster and better if you first chill the cream, beaters, and bowl.

A teaspoon of vinegar in the water used to make piecrust will make the crust flakier.

Broccoli Casserole

2 (10-ounce) packages frozen broccoli
3 tablespoons butter
3 tablespoons flour
1/2 teaspoon salt
1/4 teaspoon pepper
2 cups milk
1 cup (4 ounces) shredded cheese
Bacon slices, crisp-cooked
1/2 cup bread crumbs

Cook the broccoli using the package directions; drain. Place in a greased 8×8-inch baking dish. Melt the butter in a saucepan over low heat. Add the flour, salt and pepper. Cook until the mixture is smooth, stirring constantly. Remove from the heat. Stir in the milk. Bring to a boil. Boil for 1 minute, stirring constantly. Add the cheese. Cook until the cheese is melted, stirring constantly. Pour over the broccoli. Arrange bacon on top. Sprinkle with the bread crumbs. Bake at 350 degrees for 20 minutes.

Yield: 6 to 8 servings

IT'S BETTER TO KEEP ONE'S MOUTH SHUT AND BE THOUGHT

A FOOL THAN TO OPEN IT AND RESOLVE ALL DOUBT.

—Abraham Lincoln

Corn Pudding

2 cups corn kernels
1 tablespoon sugar
1 teaspoon salt
1/4 teaspoon pepper
1 tablespoon flour
2 tablespoons butter, melted
2 eggs, beaten
2/3 cup milk

Place the corn in a food processor and pulse until minced; do not purée. Combine the corn, sugar, salt, pepper and flour in a bowl and mix well. Stir in the butter. Add the eggs and milk and mix well. Spoon into a greased 1-quart baking dish. Bake at 350 degrees for 50 minutes or until set.

Yield: 4 servings

Creamed Potatoes

6 to 8 medium potatoes, peeled and chopped
4 teaspoons butter or margarine
4 teaspoons flour
2 cups milk
Salt and pepper to taste

Combine the potatoes and enough water to cover in a saucepan. Cook just until tender; drain. Melt the butter in a large saucepan over medium heat. Add the flour. Cook until smooth, stirring constantly. Add the milk gradually, stirring constantly. Cook until thickened, stirring constantly. Season with salt and pepper. Add the potatoes and mix well. Spoon into a serving dish. Serve immediately.

Yield: 6 servings

Peggy's Decadent Escalloped Potatoes

2 pounds potatoes
¹/2 cup (1 stick) butter or margarine, melted
1 teaspoon salt
¹/4 teaspoon pepper
1 can cream of chicken soup
2 cups (8 ounces) shredded Cheddar cheese
¹/2 cup chopped onion
2 cups sour cream
2 cups cornflakes, crushed
¹/4 cup (¹/2 stick) butter, melted

Peel the potatoes. Combine the potatoes and enough water to cover in a saucepan. Bring to a boil. Cook until tender; drain. Slice the potatoes. Combine the potatoes, ¹/2 cup margarine, salt, pepper, soup, cheese, onion and sour cream in a bowl and mix well. Spoon into a 9×13-inch baking dish. Combine the cornflakes and ¹/4 cup butter in a bowl and mix well. Sprinkle on top of the potato mixture. Bake at 350 degrees for 45 minutes or until mixture is cooked through and the top is golden brown. Serve immediately.

Yield: 12 to 15 servings

IN ORDER TO SUCCEED, YOU MUST KNOW WHAT

YOU ARE DOING, LIKE WHAT YOU ARE DOING AND

BELIEVE IN WHAT YOU ARE DOING.

—Will Rogers

Spinach Casserole

1 package frozen chopped spinach
1/2 tablespoon minced garlic, or 1/4 teaspoon garlic powder
2 eggs, beaten
1 cup sour cream
1 tablespoon flour
2 tablespoons butter, melted
1/2 cup grated Parmesan cheese

Heat the spinach and garlic in a saucepan until the spinach is thawed; drain. Remove from the heat. Stir in the eggs. Mix in the remaining ingredients. Spoon into a greased 1-quart baking dish. Bake at 350 degrees for 20 to 30 minutes.

Yield: 4 servings

Squash Casserole

6 cups sliced yellow squash
Chopped onion to taste
2 carrots, grated
1/2 cup (1 stick) margarine
1 package Stove Top Traditional Chicken Stuffing Mix
1 (10-ounce) can cream of chicken soup
8 ounces sour cream
1 pound bulk pork sausage, crumbled

Combine the squash, onion, carrots and enough water to cover in a saucepan. Bring to a boil. Boil just until the vegetables are tender. Drain, reserving 1/4 cup of the liquid. Melt the margarine in a large saucepan. Add the stuffing mix and mix well. Reserve 1 cup of the stuffing. Combine the remaining stuffing, vegetables, reserved liquid, soup, sour cream and sausage in a bowl and mix well. Spoon into a 9×13-inch baking dish. Sprinkle with the reserved stuffing mixture. Bake at 350 degrees for 30 to 40 minutes.

Yield: 10 to 12 servings

Sweet Potato Pudding

3 cups drained canned sweet potatoes
1/2 cup milk
2 eggs
1/2 teaspoon cinnamon
1/2 teaspoon nutmeg
1 teaspoon vanilla extract
1 cup sugar
1/4 cup (1/2 stick) margarine, softened
1/2 teaspoon salt
1/2 cup flour
1 cup packed brown sugar
1/2 cup chopped pecans
1/4 cup (1/2 stick) margarine, melted

Combine the sweet potatoes, milk, eggs, cinnamon, nutmeg, vanilla, sugar, softened margarine and salt in a mixing bowl. Beat until smooth. Spoon into a greased shallow 21/2- or 3-quart baking dish. Combine the flour, brown sugar, pecans and melted margarine in a bowl and mix well. Sprinkle on top of the sweet potato mixture. Bake at 350 degrees for 1 hour.

Yield: 12 servings

THERE IS LITTLE DIFFERENCE IN PEOPLE, BUT THAT LITTLE DIFFERENCE MAKES A BIG DIFFERENCE. THE LITTLE DIFFERENCE IS ATTITUDE. THE BIG DIFFERENCE IS WHETHER IT IS POSITIVE OR NEGATIVE.

—W. Clement Stone

Tomato Jam

3 cups chopped peeled tomatoes
4 cups sugar
2 tablespoons lemon juice
1 (6-ounce) package Jell-O Brand Strawberry Flavor Gelatin

Combine the tomatoes, sugar and lemon juice in a saucepan. Bring to a boil, stirring frequently. Boil for 20 to 25 minutes, stirring frequently. Sprinkle with the Jell-O and stir to mix well. Spoon into hot sterilized 1-pint jars, leaving $1/2$ inch headspace. Process in a boiling water bath for 10 minutes. You may spoon the mixture into freezer containers and freeze.

Yield: 2 (1-pint) jars

Garlic Cheese Grits

1 cup quick-cooking grits
1 cup (4 ounces) shredded American cheese
$1/2$ cup (1 stick) butter or margarine
1 teaspoon garlic salt
1 egg
$1/4$ to $1/3$ cup milk

Cook the grits using the package directions. Add the cheese, butter and garlic salt. Cook until the cheese and butter are melted, stirring constantly. Beat the egg in a 1-cup measure. Add enough milk to measure $1/2$ cup. Add the egg mixture to the grits mixture and mix well. Spoon into a greased $11/2$-quart baking dish. Bake at 350 degrees for 20 to 25 minutes or until bubbly around the edges. Sprinkle with additional cheese if desired.

Yield: 4 to 6 servings

Jan's Stuffing

3 cups chopped celery
1 cup chopped Vidalia onion
1/2 cup chopped carrot
2 tablespoons butter or margarine
1 cup sliced mushrooms
1/2 cup chopped almonds
1 cup cooked crumbled sausage
6 quarts dry white and/or rye bread cubes
1/2 tablespoon salt
1 teaspoon poultry seasoning
1/2 teaspoon McCormick's Garlic Herb Seasoning or
McCormick's Parsley Patch Garlic
2 cans (or more) chicken broth
2 eggs

Sauté the celery, onion and carrot in the butter in a skillet just until tender. Add the mushrooms, almonds, sausage, bread, salt, poultry seasoning and Garlic Herb Seasoning and mix well. Stir in the broth. Cook over low heat for 6 minutes, stirring frequently. Spoon into a baking dish. Bake at 350 degrees until the top is browned.

Yield: 4 servings

Note: The chicken broth eliminates the need to put the stuffing in the turkey or chicken.

Pretzels

1¹/2 cups flour
2 teaspoons baking powder
1 teaspoon sugar
¹/2 teaspoon salt
²/3 cup milk
2 tablespoons butter or margarine, softened
1 egg
2 tablespoons water
Coarse or kosher salt

Combine the flour, baking powder, sugar and salt in a bowl and mix with a fork. Add the milk and butter and mix until a soft dough forms. Shape into a ball on a floured surface. Knead the dough 10 times or until smooth by pressing with heels of hands and folding the dough in half.

Divide the dough into 2 equal portions. Reserve 1 portion of the dough, covering with plastic wrap. Cut the remaining dough into 8 equal portions. Roll each portion into a 12-inch rope. Twist each rope into a pretzel shape. Arrange the pretzels pinched edge down on a greased baking sheet. Repeat procedure with the reserved dough.

Combine the egg and 2 tablespoons water in a bowl and beat with a fork. Brush the pretzels with the egg mixture. Sprinkle lightly with coarse salt.

Bake at 400 degrees for 20 to 25 minutes or until golden brown. Remove to wire racks using a spatula; cool completely. Store in a tightly covered container.

Yield: 16 pretzels

Dinner Rolls

1 cup hot water
1 teaspoon salt
6 tablespoons shortening
1/4 cup sugar
1 envelope dry yeast
2 tablespoons warm water
1 egg, beaten
3 to 3 1/2 cups flour

Combine the hot water, salt, shortening and sugar in a large mixing bowl and mix well. Cool to lukewarm. Soften the yeast in the warm water in a bowl. Add to the cooled mixture. Add the egg and half the flour and beat well. Stir in enough flour to make a soft dough. Grease the top of the dough. Let rise, covered, in a warm place for 45 to 60 minutes or until doubled in bulk. Punch the dough down. Shape into rolls. Arrange on greased baking sheets. Let rise, covered, in a warm place until doubled in bulk. Bake at 400 degrees for 15 minutes or until browned. You may store the unrisen dough, covered, in the refrigerator and use as needed. Shape desired amount of dough into rolls. Arrange on greased baking sheets. Let rise, covered, in a warm place for 2 to 3 hours or until doubled in bulk. Bake at 425 degrees for 12 to 15 minutes or until browned.

To make *Cinnamon Rolls*, let the dough rise, covered, in a warm place for 45 to 60 minutes or until doubled in bulk. Roll into a rectangle on a floured surface. Sprinkle with cinnamon and brown sugar. Roll as for a jelly roll. Cut into 1/2-inch slices. Arrange on greased baking sheets. Let rise, covered, until doubled in bulk. Bake at 350 degrees for 20 minutes. Frost cooled rolls as desired.

To make *Pepperoni Bread*, let the dough rise, covered, in a warm place for 45 to 60 minutes or until doubled in bulk. Roll into a rectangle on a floured surface. Brush with vegetable oil and sprinkle with seasoned salt. Top with pepperoni. Roll as for a jelly roll, sealing the edge and ends. Place seam side down on a greased baking sheet. Bake for 20 minutes or until browned.

Yield: 3 dozen rolls

Pepperoni Bread

1 loaf Rich's Frozen Bread Dough
1 to 2 cups thinly sliced pepperoni
1/2 cup (2 ounces) shredded mozzarella cheese
Grated Parmesan cheese
Grated Romano cheese

Thaw the dough for 2¹/₂ to 3 hours or until soft. Roll the dough into a 10×14-inch rectangle.

Arrange the pepperoni on top of the dough, making 4 rows with 8 slices per row. Sprinkle with the cheese. Roll the dough to enclose the filling, sealing the seam and ends. Place on a baking sheet. Bake at 350 degrees for 30 to 35 minutes or until browned and crusty. Serve with pizza sauce.

Yield: 1 loaf

Note: You may add minced garlic, chopped onion, or chopped red bell pepper with the pepperoni.

IT IS A MISTAKE TO LOOK TOO FAR AHEAD. ONLY ONE LINK

OF THE CHAIN OF DESTINY CAN BE HANDLED AT A TIME.

—Winston Churchill

Thanksgiving Cranberry Nut Bread

1/4 cup (1/2 stick) butter, softened
1/3 to 1/2 cup packed brown sugar
1/3 to 1/2 cup molasses
2 eggs
1/2 cup orange juice
1/2 cup buttermilk
1 1/2 cups all-purpose flour
1 1/2 cups whole wheat flour
1/3 cup dry milk powder
3 teaspoons baking powder
1 teaspoon baking soda
1/2 teaspoon salt
1 teaspoon nutmeg
1 teaspoon allspice
1 teaspoon grated orange zest
1 cup chopped nuts (walnuts or pecans preferred)
2 cups cranberry halves

Beat the butter, brown sugar and molasses in a mixing bowl until creamy.
Beat in the eggs, orange juice and buttermilk.

Combine the all-purpose flour, whole wheat flour, milk powder, baking
powder, baking soda, salt, nutmeg, allspice, orange zest and nuts in a bowl
and mix well. Add to the egg mixture gradually, beating constantly. Fold
in the cranberries. Spoon into a greased and floured large loaf pan.

Bake at 350 degrees for 1 to 1 1/4 hours or until the bread tests done.
Remove to a wire rack to cool completely. You may line the greased loaf
pan with waxed paper and omit the flour. You may bake the bread in
2 medium loaf pans and adjust the baking time.

Yield: 1 large loaf or 2 medium loaves

Note: This bread tastes best the next day. Wrap securely
to maintain freshness.

Zucchini Bread

3 eggs
2 cups sugar
2 teaspoons vanilla extract
1 cup vegetable oil
3 cups shredded zucchini
1 teaspoon salt
1 teaspoon cinnamon
1 cup chopped nuts
1/2 cup shredded coconut
3 cups flour
1 teaspoon baking soda
1 teaspoon baking powder

Beat the eggs in a large mixing bowl. Add the sugar, vanilla, oil, zucchini, salt, cinnamon, nuts, coconut, flour, baking soda and baking powder in the order listed, mixing well after each addition. Spoon into 2 greased loaf pans. Bake at 350 degrees for 30 to 35 minutes or until a wooden pick inserted in the center comes out clean.

Yield: 2 loaves

A FRESH BAY LEAF INSIDE YOUR FLOUR CANISTER

WILL KEEP THE BUGS AWAY.

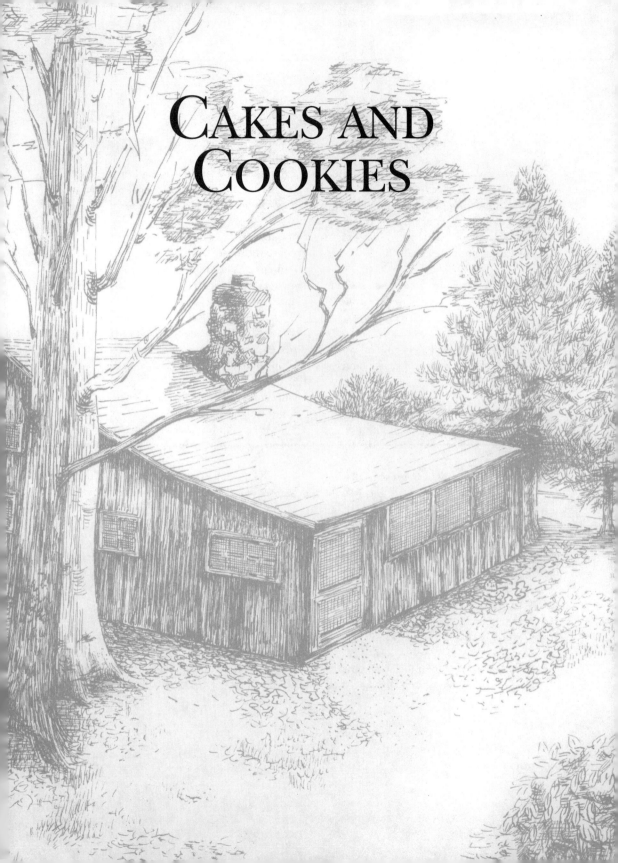

CAKES AND COOKIES

Cooking Ideas

To preserve leftover egg yolks for future use, place them in a small bowl and add two tablespoons of vegetable oil. Then place in the refrigerator. The egg yolks will remain soft and fresh. Egg yolks kept in this way can be used in many ways.

To keep egg yolks from crumbling when slicing hard-cooked eggs, wet the knife before each cut.

Bread crumbs added to scrambled eggs will improve the flavor and make larger helpings possible.

A tablespoon of vinegar added to the water when poaching eggs will help set the whites so they will not spread.

When cooking eggs, it helps prevent cracking if you wet the shells in cold water before placing them in boiling water.

Add a little vinegar to the water when an egg cracks during boiling. It will help seal the egg.

Meringue will not shrink if you spread it on the pie so that it touches the crust on each side and bake it in a moderate oven.

When you cook eggs in the shell, put a big teaspoonful of salt in the water. The shell will not crack.

Place eggs in a pan of warm water before using as this releases all of the egg white from the shells.

Egg whites for meringue should be brought to room temperature before beating, then they can beaten to greater volume.

If you want to make a pecan pie and do not have any pecans, substitute crushed cornflakes. They will rise to the top the same as nuts and give a delicious flavor and a crunchy surface.

To prevent the crust of a cream pie from becoming soggy, sprinkle the crust with confectioners' sugar.

Cut drinking straws into short lengths and insert through slits in piecrusts to prevent juice from running over in the oven and to permit steam to escape.

Put a layer of marshmallows in the bottom of a pumpkin pie, then add the filling. You will have a nice topping as the marshmallows will come to the top.

If the juice from your apple pie runs over in the oven, shake some salt on it, which causes the juice to burn to a crisp so it can be removed.

Use vegetable oil in waffles and hot cakes in place of shortening—no extra pan or bowl to melt the shortening and no waiting.

Gooey Butter Cake

1/2 cup (1 stick) butter or margarine, melted
1 egg, beaten
1 (2-layer) package cake mix (any flavor)
8 ounces cream cheese, softened
2 eggs
2 cups confectioners' sugar

Combine the butter and 1 egg in a mixing bowl and beat well. Add the cake mix and blend until mixture resembles cookie dough. Press onto the bottom and 1 inch up the sides of a 9×13-inch cake pan.

Combine the cream cheese, 2 eggs and confectioners' sugar in a mixing bowl and beat well. Spread over the top of the cake mix layer. Bake at 350 degrees for 40 minutes.

Yield: 15 servings

Note: This is always a favorite for all ages.

AMERICA IS NOT LIKE A BLANKET—ONE PIECE OF

UNBROKEN CLOTH. AMERICA IS MORE LIKE A QUILT—MANY

PATCHES, MANY PIECES, MANY COLORS, MANY SIZES, ALL

WOVEN TOGETHER BY A COMMON THREAD.

—The Rev. Jesse L. Jackson

Mrs. D's Chocolate Cake

2 cups each flour and sugar
1/2 cup (1 stick) margarine
1/4 cup baking cocoa
1/2 cup Crisco All-Vegetable Shortening
1 cup water
1/2 cup buttermilk
2 eggs
1 teaspoon each vanilla extract and baking soda
Chocolate Topping

Combine the flour and sugar in a bowl and mix well. Combine the margarine, baking cocoa, shortening and water in a saucepan. Bring to a boil, stirring constantly. Add to the flour mixture and mix well. Add the buttermilk, eggs, vanilla and baking soda and mix well. Spread in a 9×13-inch cake pan. Bake at 400 degrees for 20 minutes; cool completely. Pour the warm Chocolate Topping over the cake and spread evenly.

Yield: 16 servings

Chocolate Topping

1/2 cup (1 stick) margarine
6 tablespoons milk
1/4 cup baking cocoa
1 (1-pound) package confectioners' sugar
1 cup chopped walnuts
1 teaspoon vanilla extract

Combine the margarine, milk and baking cocoa in a saucepan. Bring to a boil, stirring constantly. Remove from the heat. Stir in the confectioners' sugar until smooth. Add the walnuts and vanilla and mix well.

Note: This can be made into brownies by baking in a
10×15-inch baking pan.

Red Velvet Cake

1/2 cup (1 stick) margarine, softened
1 (2-layer) package white cake mix
1 (4-ounce) package chocolate instant pudding mix
4 eggs
1 cup water
2 ounces red food coloring
1 tablespoon vinegar
1/2 tablespoon baking soda
Red Velvet Icing

Cream the margarine in a large mixing bowl. Add the cake mix and pudding mix and mix well. Add the eggs, water and food coloring. Beat for 3 minutes. Stir in the vinegar and baking soda. Pour into 2 greased and floured 9-inch cake pans. Bake at 350 degrees for 30 to 35 minutes or until the cake tests done. Cool in the pan for 10 minutes. Remove to wire racks to cool completely. Spread the Red Velvet Icing between the layers and over the top and side of the cooled cake.

Yield: 10 to 12 servings

Red Velvet Icing

1/2 cup (1 stick) butter or margarine, softened
1/2 cup Crisco All-Vegetable Shortening
1 cup sugar
3 tablespoons flour
2/3 cup milk
1 tablespoon vanilla extract

Cream the butter, shortening and sugar in a mixing bowl. Add the flour 1 tablespoon at a time, beating constantly. Beat in the milk and vanilla. Beat for 12 minutes.

Bet's Coca-Cola Cake

2 cups flour
2 cups sugar
1 teaspoon baking soda
1 cup (2 sticks) margarine
1 1/2 cups miniature marshmallows
1 cup Coca-Cola
3 tablespoons baking cocoa
2 eggs, beaten
1/2 teaspoon vanilla extract
1/2 cup sour cream
1 can Betty Crocker Chocolate Frosting

Sift the flour, sugar and baking soda into a bowl. Combine the margarine, marshmallows, Coca-Cola and baking cocoa in a saucepan. Cook over low heat until the marshmallows are melted, stirring constantly. Add to the flour mixture and mix well. Stir in the eggs, vanilla and sour cream. Pour into a 9-inch cake pan. Bake at 350 degrees for 30 to 35 minutes or until the cake tests done. Cool in the pan for 10 minutes. Remove to a wire rack to cool completely. Spread the frosting over the top and side of the cooled cake.

Yield: 4 to 6 servings

WHERE THERE IS NO VISION, THE PEOPLE PERISH.

—*Proverbs 29:18*

Fruit Cocktail Cake

1¹/2 cups sugar
2 eggs
2 cups sifted flour
2 teaspoons baking soda
¹/2 teaspoon salt
1¹/2 cups undrained fruit cocktail
¹/4 cup packed brown sugar
¹/4 cup chopped pecans
Brown Sugar Topping

Beat the sugar and eggs in a mixing bowl. Sift the flour, baking soda and salt together. Add to the sugar mixture alternately with the fruit cocktail, mixing well after each addition. Spoon into a greased and floured 9×13-inch cake pan. Sprinkle with the brown sugar and pecans. Bake at 350 degrees for 40 minutes. Pour the Brown Sugar Topping evenly over the warm cake.

Yield: 15 servings

Brown Sugar Topping

¹/4 cup packed brown sugar
³/4 cup sugar
¹/2 cup evaporated milk
¹/4 cup (¹/2 stick) margarine
1 teaspoon vanilla extract

Combine the brown sugar, sugar, evaporated milk and margarine in a saucepan. Bring to a boil, stirring constantly. Boil for 1 minute, stirring constantly. Remove from the heat. Stir in the vanilla.

French Angel Food Cake

1 package angel food cake mix
1 (3-ounce) package lemon Jell-O Brand
Cook & Serve Pudding & Pie Filling
1 cup water
1/2 cup sugar
2 tablespoons lemon juice
1 quart heavy whipping cream
1/4 cup sugar
1 teaspoon vanilla extract

Prepare and bake the angel food cake using the package directions; cool completely.

Combine the pudding mix, water, 1/2 cup sugar and lemon juice in a saucepan. Cook until thickened, stirring constantly; cool completely. Chill, covered, in the refrigerator.

Combine the whipping cream, 1/4 cup sugar and vanilla in a mixing bowl and beat until stiff peaks form. Divide into 2 equal portions.

Cut the cake into 3 horizontal slices. Combine the pudding mix mixture and 1 portion of the whipping cream mixture in a bowl and mix well. Spread between the layers of the cake. Spread the remaining whipping cream mixture over the top of the cake. Chill, covered, until serving time. Garnish with pansies.

Yield: 10 servings

Note: This delicious cake is best if made the night before.

Oatmeal Cake

1 cup rolled oats
1/2 cup (1 stick) margarine
1 1/2 cups boiling water
1 cup sugar
1 cup packed brown sugar
1 1/2 cups flour
1 teaspoon cinnamon
1 teaspoon baking soda
1/2 teaspoon salt
2 eggs
1 teaspoon vanilla extract
Coconut Topping

Combine the oats, margarine and boiling water in a bowl. Let stand, covered, for 20 minutes. Stir in the sugar, brown sugar, flour, cinnamon, baking soda and salt. Add the eggs and vanilla and mix well. Spoon into a greased and floured 9×13-inch cake pan. Bake at 350 degrees for 35 to 40 minutes or until the cake tests done. Spread the Coconut Topping over the warm cake. Broil for 3 minutes or until the topping is bubbly.

Yield: 15 servings

Coconut Topping

2/3 cup packed brown sugar
1/4 cup evaporated milk
1 cup Rice Krispies
1/2 cup chopped nuts
6 tablespoons margarine, softened
1 teaspoon vanilla extract
1 cup flaked coconut

Combine the brown sugar, milk, cereal, nuts, margarine, vanilla and coconut in a bowl and mix well.

Peach Cake

1 (2-layer) package yellow or butter cake mix
2 tablespoons butter
2 tablespoons brown sugar
2 tablespoons peach preserves
Thinly sliced peaches
Whipped cream or whipped topping

Prepare and bake the cake using the package directions for 2 round layers. Cool in the pans for 10 minutes. Remove to wire racks to cool completely. Combine the butter, brown sugar and preserves in a saucepan. Cook until the mixture is melted, stirring constantly. Place 1 cake layer on a serving plate. Pour half the butter mixture evenly over the cake layer. Arrange peaches on top. Place the second cake layer on top of the peaches. Pour the remaining butter mixture evenly over the top. Arrange peaches on top. Spread whipped cream over the top and side of the cake. Garnish with peaches.

Yield: 12 servings

Note: Very easy, elegant, and moist.

WE EACH NEED TO ADMIT WHEN WE ARE WRONG

AND BE HUMBLE WHEN WE'RE RIGHT.

—Johnetta B. Cole

Watergate Cake

1 (2-layer) package white cake mix
1 (4-ounce) package pistachio instant pudding mix
3 eggs
1 cup vegetable oil
1 cup club soda
1/2 cup chopped pecans or walnuts
Watergate Frosting

Combine the cake mix, pudding mix, eggs, oil and club soda in a mixing bowl. Beat at medium speed for 2 minutes. Fold in the pecans. Pour into a greased and floured 10-inch tube pan. Bake at 350 degrees for 45 to 55 minutes. Cool in the pan for 10 minutes. Remove to a wire rack to cool completely. Spread Watergate Frosting over the top and side of the cooled cake. You may omit the frosting and garnish the cake with additional pecans.

Yield: 8 to 10 servings

Watergate Frosting

1 (4-ounce) package pistachio instant pudding mix
1 envelope Dream Whip Whipped Topping Mix
1 1/2 cups cold milk

Combine the pudding mix, whipped topping mix and milk in a mixing bowl. Beat until light and fluffy.

Pumpkin Roll

2/3 cup pumpkin purée
3 eggs
1/2 teaspoon cinnamon
1 cup sugar
1 teaspoon baking soda
3/4 cup flour
1 teaspoon salt
Confectioners' sugar for dusting
8 ounces cream cheese, softened
1 teaspoon vanilla extract
2 tablespoons butter
1 cup confectioners' sugar

Combine the pumpkin, eggs, cinnamon, sugar, baking soda, flour and salt in a mixing bowl and beat well. Line a 10×15-inch cake pan with waxed paper. Grease the waxed paper. Pour the pumpkin mixture into the cake pan, spreading evenly. Bake at 375 degrees for 15 minutes. Dust a clean kitchen towel with confectioners' sugar. Invert the cake onto the towel. Remove the waxed paper and trim the edges of the cake. Roll the warm cake in the towel as for a jelly roll from the short side. Chill for 1 hour. Unroll the cake carefully and remove the towel. Combine the cream cheese, vanilla, butter and 1 cup confectioners' sugar in a mixing bowl and beat well. Spread the filling evenly over the cake and reroll. Place seam side down on a serving plate. Chill, covered, until serving time.

Yield: 1 cake roll

The Girl Scout Cookie Recipe

1 cup butter or substitute, softened
1 cup sugar
2 eggs
2 tablespoons milk
1 teaspoon vanilla
2 cups flour
2 teaspoons baking powder

Beat the butter and sugar together in a mixing bowl until smooth and creamy. Add well beaten eggs, then milk, flavoring, flour and baking powder. Roll thin and bake in quick oven. (A "quick" oven would be about 375 degrees for 10 minutes.) Sprinkle sugar on top.

Yield: 6 to 7 dozen cookies

Note: In 1922, the Girl Scouts printed this sugar cookie recipe for Girl Scouts to make and sell. This recipe was from the mini page of the *Winchester Star*.

DON'T BE AFRAID TO TAKE A BIG STEP WHEN ONE IS

INDICATED. YOU CAN'T CROSS A CHASM IN TWO SMALL STEPS.

—David Loyd George

Old-Time Soft Sugar Cookies

2 cups sugar
2 eggs
1 cup shortening
2 cups sour cream or buttermilk
2 teaspoons vanilla extract
6¹/₂ cups flour
1 teaspoon baking soda
2 teaspoons baking powder
1 teaspoon salt
Sugar and cinnamon (optional)

Cream the sugar, eggs and shortening in a mixing bowl. Beat in the sour cream and vanilla. Sift the flour, baking soda, baking powder and salt together. Add to the sugar mixture and mix well. Pat ¹/₈ inch thick on a lightly floured surface. Cut with cookie cutters. Place 2 inches apart on nonstick cookie sheets. Sprinkle with sugar and cinnamon. Bake at 350 degrees for 15 to 20 minutes. Cool on cookie sheets for 2 minutes. Remove to wire racks to cool completely.

Yield: 5 to 6 dozen cookies

Note: The cookie dough may be very moist. If so, add a little more flour. Do not use a rolling pin. Flatten dough with hands.

> *EXCELLENCE IS NOT AN ACCOMPLISHMENT. IT IS A*
>
> *SPIRIT, A NEVER-ENDING PROCESS.*
>
> —*Lawrence M. Miller*

Sugar Cookies

1¹/2 cups sugar
1 cup lard
1 egg
2 teaspoons vanilla extract
1 cup sour milk
1/2 teaspoon salt
1 teaspoon baking soda
2 teaspoons baking powder
5 to 6 cups flour

Beat the sugar and lard in a mixing bowl until well mixed. Beat in the egg. Add the vanilla and milk and mix well. Beat in the salt, baking soda, baking powder and enough flour to make a soft dough. Roll 1/8 inch thick on a lightly floured surface. Cut with cookie cutters. Place 2 inches apart on greased cookie sheets. Bake at 375 degrees for 10 to 12 minutes. Cool on cookie sheets for 2 minutes. Remove to wire racks to cool.

Yield: 5 to 6 dozen cookies

Flint Central High Cookies

1 cup each sugar and packed brown sugar
2/3 cup peanut butter
2/3 cup Crisco All-Vegetable Shortening
1 teaspoon salt
2 eggs, beaten
2 cups flour
1 teaspoon vanilla extract

Combine all the ingredients in a bowl and mix well. Shape into 1- to 1¹/2-inch balls. Place 2 inches apart on nonstick cookie sheets. Flatten with a fork. Bake at 350 degrees until browned.

Yield: 2 to 3 dozen cookies

Chocolate Chip Cookies

1 cup (2 sticks) butter or margarine, softened
3/4 cup each sugar and packed light brown sugar
1 teaspoon vanilla extract
2 eggs
2 1/4 cups unsifted flour
1 teaspoon baking soda
1/2 teaspoon salt (optional)
2 cups (12 ounces) semisweet chocolate chips

Beat the first 4 ingredients in a mixing bowl until creamy. Beat in the eggs. Stir in the dry ingredients. Beat into the creamed mixture gradually. Stir in the chocolate chips. Drop by teaspoonfuls 2 inches apart onto ungreased cookie sheets. Bake at 375 degrees for 8 to 10 minutes. Cool on cookie sheets for 2 minutes. Remove to wire racks to cool completely.

Yield: 6 dozen cookies

Ginger Crinkles

1 1/2 cups vegetable oil
2 cups sugar
2 eggs
1/2 cup molasses
4 cups flour
4 teaspoons baking soda
1 teaspoon salt
2 teaspoons each cinnamon and ginger

Beat the oil and sugar in a mixing bowl. Add the remaining ingredients. Shape into 2-inch balls. Dip in additional sugar. Place 2 inches apart on ungreased cookie sheets. Bake at 350 degrees for 10 minutes. Cool on cookie sheets for 2 minutes. Remove to wire racks to cool completely.

Yield: 2 dozen cookies

All-American Brownies

¹/4 cup (¹/2 stick) unsalted butter
2 ounces unsweetened chocolate, chopped
8 ounces bittersweet chocolate, chopped
2 eggs
1 cup sugar
2 teaspoons vanilla extract
¹/8 teaspoon salt
¹/2 cup flour
1 cup chopped walnuts or pecans

Combine the butter and chocolate in a saucepan. Cook over low heat until melted, stirring constantly. Whisk the eggs and sugar in a large bowl. Stir in the vanilla and salt. Add the chocolate mixture and mix well. Stir in the flour and walnuts. Spread evenly in a buttered 8×8-inch baking pan. Bake at 325 degrees for 40 minutes. Cool in the pan on a wire rack.

Yield: 9 brownies

CHILL DOUGH FIRST TO KEEP DROP COOKIES

FROM SPREADING.

Peanut Butter Chip Brownies

3/4 cup Hershey's Baking Cocoa
1/2 teaspoon baking soda
1/3 cup margarine, melted
1/2 cup boiling water
2 cups sugar
2 eggs
1/3 cup margarine, melted
1 1/2 cups flour
1 teaspoon vanilla extract
1/4 teaspoon salt
1 (12-ounce) package Reese's Peanut Butter Chips

Combine the baking cocoa and baking soda in a large bowl and mix well. Add 1/3 cup margarine and mix well. Add the boiling water and stir until the mixture thickens. Add the sugar, eggs and 1/3 cup margarine and stir until smooth. Add the flour, vanilla and salt and mix well. Stir in the peanut butter chips. Pour into a lightly greased 9×13-inch baking pan. Bake at 350 degrees for 30 minutes. Cool completely on a wire rack. Cut into bars.

Yield: 2 dozen brownies

Note: This is from a 1984 cookbook. It was submitted by Jessica Faupel, now 25 years old and receiving her Ph.D. at Mayo next year.

WE MUST BECOME THE CHANGE WE WANT TO SEE.

—Mahatma Gandhi

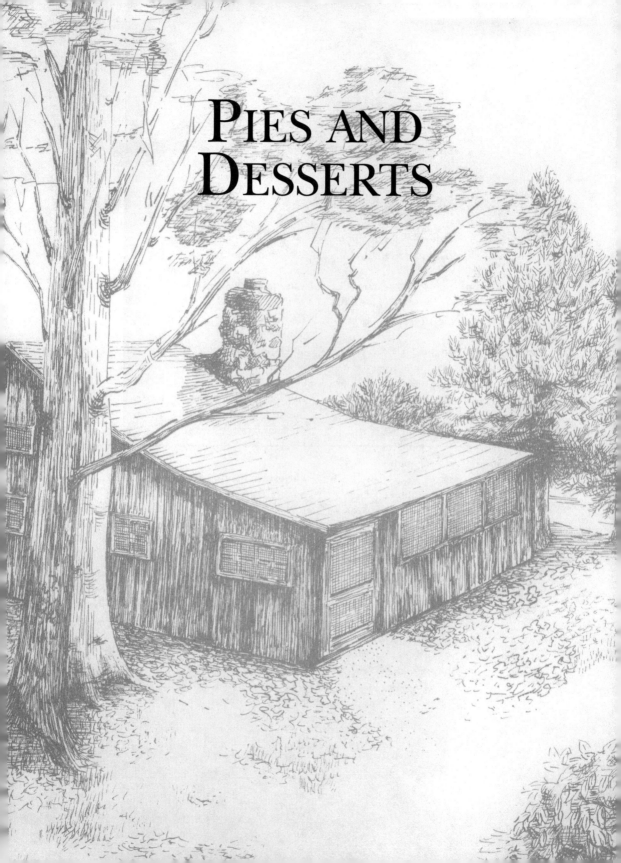

PIES AND DESSERTS

Worth Remembering

Sweet potatoes will not turn dark if put in salt water (five teaspoons to one quart of water) immediately after peeling.

Potatoes soaked in salt water for 20 minutes before baking will bake more rapidly.

Let raw potatoes stand in cold water for at least an hour before frying to improve the crispness of French-fried potatoes.

The skins will remain tender if you wrap potatoes in aluminum foil to bake them. They are attractively served in the foil, too (not for microwaves).

If you add a little milk to the water in which cauliflower is cooking, the cauliflower will remain attractively white.

When and how you add salt in cooking is important. To blend with soups and sauces, put the salt in early. But add salt to meats just before removing from the stove. In cake ingredients, salt can be mixed with the eggs. When cooking vegetables, always salt the water in which they are cooked. Put salt in the pan with frying fish.

You can get more juice from a dried up lemon if you heat it for five minutes in boiling water before you squeeze it.

The white membranes on oranges are easy to remove—for fancy desserts or salads—by soaking the oranges in boiling water for five minutes before peeling them.

If it's important to you to get walnut meats out whole, soak the nuts overnight in salt water before you crack them.

If whipping cream looks as though it is not going to whip, add three or four drops of lemon juice or a bit of plain gelatin powder to it and it probably will.

Dip your bananas in lemon juice right after they are peeled. They will not turn dark and the faint flavor of lemon really adds quite a bit. The same may be done with apples.

Use greased muffin tins as molds when baking stuffed green bell peppers.

A few drops of lemon juice in the water will whiten boiled potatoes.

When cooking cabbage, place a small tin cup or can half full of vinegar on the stove near the cabbage, and it will absorb all the odor from the cabbage.

Chocolate Cream Pie

8 ounces cream cheese, softened
1/2 cup milk
1 (6-ounce) package chocolate instant pudding mix
2 cups milk
Graham cracker pie shell
Cool Whip Whipped Topping

Combine the cream cheese and 1/2 cup milk in a large mixing bowl and beat until blended. Add the pudding mix and 2 cups milk. Beat for 4 to 5 minutes. Pour into the pie shell. Spread the whipped topping over the top. Chill until serving time.

Yield: 6 to 8 servings

Dixie Pecan Pie

3 eggs
2 tablespoons each sugar and flour
2 cups Karo Dark Corn Syrup
1 teaspoon vanilla extract
1/4 teaspoon salt
1 cup (or more) pecan pieces
1 unbaked (9-inch) pie shell

Beat the eggs in a large mixing bowl until light. Combine the sugar and flour and mix well. Add to the eggs and beat well. Add the corn syrup, vanilla, salt and pecans and mix well. Pour into the pie shell. Bake at 425 degrees for 10 minutes. Reduce the oven temperature to 325 degrees. Bake for 45 minutes or until set.

Yield: 8 servings

Note: This recipe is from the Helen Corbitt cookbook. It's really good, not overly sweet.

Four-Layer Pie

1¹/₂ sticks (³/₄ cup) butter or margarine, softened
1¹/₂ cups flour
³/₄ cup pecan pieces
9 ounces Cool Whip Whipped Topping
8 ounces cream cheese, softened
1 cup confectioners' sugar
1 (4-ounce) package vanilla instant pudding mix
1 (4-ounce) package chocolate instant pudding mix
3 cups milk
9 ounces Cool Whip Whipped Topping

Combine the butter, flour and pecans in a bowl and mix with a fork. Press onto the bottom and up the side of a 9-inch pie plate. Bake at 375 degrees for 20 to 25 minutes; cool. Combine 9 ounces whipped topping, cream cheese and confectioners' sugar in a mixing bowl and beat well. Spread over the piecrust. Combine the vanilla pudding mix, chocolate pudding mix and milk in a bowl and mix well. Spread over the whipped topping mixture. Spread 9 ounces whipped topping over the top of the pie. Chill until serving time.

Yield: 6 to 8 servings

Impossible Pumpkin Pie

3/4 cup sugar
1/2 cup Bisquick Baking Mix
1 (16-ounce) can pumpkin purée
2 eggs
2 tablespoons butter or margarine, softened
2 1/2 teaspoons pumpkin pie spice
1 (13-ounce) can evaporated milk
2 teaspoons vanilla extract

Combine the sugar, baking mix, pumpkin, eggs, butter, pumpkin pie spice, evaporated milk and vanilla in a mixing bowl. Beat for 2 minutes or until smooth. May process in a blender for 1 minute or until smooth. Pour into a greased 9- or 10-inch pie plate. Bake for 50 to 55 minutes or until a knife inserted in the center of the pie comes out clean.

Yield: 6 to 8 servings

Note: It is not necessary to put this in a pie shell.

PLACE A BAKING SHEET OR PAN UNDER PIES WHILE BAKING

TO ASSURE THE BOTTOM CRUST WILL BROWN.

Strawberry Pie

1 cup flour
1/4 cup unpacked brown sugar
1/2 cup (1 stick) margarine, softened
1/4 cup chopped pecans
1 cup sugar
3 tablespoons cornstarch
12 ounces 7-Up
1/4 teaspoon salt
6 drops (about) of red food coloring
Dash of cinnamon
3 drops of strawberry oil
Kirsch or almond extract to taste
1 quart (about) strawberries, sliced

Combine the flour, brown sugar and margarine in a bowl and mix until crumbly. Add the pecans and mix well. You may process the ingredients in a food processor. Press the mixture onto the bottom and up the side of a 10-inch pie plate; chill. Bake at 375 degrees for 12 to 15 minutes; cool.

Combine the sugar, cornstarch, 7-Up and salt in a microwave-safe bowl. Microwave for 2 minutes; stir. Repeat the procedure. Microwave for 1 to 1 1/2 minutes or just until the glaze is thickened; stir. Add the food coloring and cinnamon and mix well. Stir in the strawberry oil and kirsch.

Spread a small amount of the glaze over the bottom of the piecrust. Combine the remaining glaze and strawberries in a bowl and mix well. Spoon into the piecrust. Chill until serving time.

Yield: 8 servings

Cheesecake

1¹/₂ cups graham cracker crumbs
¹/₂ teaspoon cinnamon
3 tablespoons sugar
¹/₄ cup (¹/₂ stick) butter, melted
24 ounces cream cheese, softened
1 cup sugar
¹/₂ teaspoon vanilla extract
4 eggs
1 tablespoon lemon juice
1 teaspoon grated lemon zest
1 cup sour cream
1 teaspoon vanilla extract
1 tablespoon sugar

Combine the graham cracker crumbs, cinnamon, 3 tablespoons sugar and butter in a bowl and mix well. Press onto the bottom of a greased springform pan. Bake at 300 degrees on the top oven rack for 10 minutes.

Combine the cream cheese, 1 cup sugar and ¹/₂ teaspoon vanilla in a mixing bowl and beat well. Add the eggs 1 at a time, beating well after each addition. Beat in the lemon juice and lemon zest. Pour into the prepared pan. Bake for 45 minutes.

Mix the sour cream, 1 teaspoon vanilla and 1 tablespoon sugar in a bowl. Spread over the top of the cheesecake. Bake for 10 minutes; cool. Chill until serving time.

Yield: 6 servings

Note: This cheesecake may be topped with blueberry or cherry pie filling.

Mini Cheesecakes

24 vanilla wafers
16 ounces cream cheese, softened
1/2 cup sugar
2 eggs
1 teaspoon vanilla extract
Cherry or blueberry pie filling

Place a foil liner in each of 24 muffin cups. Place a vanilla wafer in the bottom of each liner. Combine the cream cheese, sugar, eggs and vanilla in a mixing bowl. Beat at medium speed until blended. Fill the prepared muffin cups half full. Bake at 325 degrees for 25 minutes; cool. Top with cherry pie filling.

Yield: 24 servings

Note: These freeze well.

Baked Apples

5 medium McIntosh or Golden Delicious apples
1/2 cup (1 stick) margarine
1 1/2 cups packed brown sugar
3 to 4 tablespoons flour
2 cups milk
1 teaspoon vanilla extract

Peel and core the apples. Cut the apples into halves. Arrange in a 9×13-inch baking dish. Combine the margarine, brown sugar, flour and milk in a heavy saucepan. Cook over medium heat to a pudding consistency, stirring constantly. Remove from the heat. Stir in the vanilla. Pour over the apples. Bake at 350 degrees for 35 minutes or until the apples are tender.

Yield: 6 servings

Apple Dumpling Dessert

2 cups flour
1 cup milk
1½ teaspoons baking powder
1 cup sugar, or ¼ cup fructose
½ teaspoon salt
6 cups sliced apples
½ cup (1 stick) butter
1 teaspoon cinnamon
¾ cup packed light brown sugar

Combine the flour, milk, baking powder, sugar and salt in a bowl and mix well. Pour over the apples in a bowl and mix gently. Spoon into a greased 9×13-inch baking pan. Combine the butter, cinnamon and brown sugar in a saucepan. Cook until syrupy, stirring constantly. Pour evenly over the apple mixture. Bake at 350 degrees for 1 hour.

Yield: 12 to 15 servings

Apple Crisp

6 medium apples, peeled and sliced
1 cup each flour and sugar
1 teaspoon baking powder
½ teaspoon salt
1 egg
Cinnamon
½ cup (1 stick) margarine, melted

Place the apples in a lightly greased 9×9-inch baking dish. Mix the flour, sugar, baking powder, salt and egg in a bowl until crumbly. Spoon over the apples. Sprinkle with cinnamon. Pour the margarine over the top. Bake at 350 degrees for 35 to 45 minutes or until the apples are tender.

Yield: 9 servings

Banana Split Dessert

3/4 cup (1 1/2 sticks) butter, melted
3 cups graham cracker crumbs
1 cup (2 sticks) butter, softened
2 cups confectioners' sugar
2 eggs
1 teaspoon vanilla extract
6 or 7 bananas, sliced
1 large can crushed pineapple, drained
1 large package Cool Whip Whipped Topping
1/2 cup chopped nuts
1 jar maraschino cherries, cut into halves

Combine 3/4 cup butter and graham cracker crumbs in a bowl and mix well. Press onto the bottom of a 9×13-inch pan.

Combine 1 cup butter, confectioners' sugar, eggs and vanilla in a mixing bowl and beat until smooth. Pour the filling over the crust. Let stand for 20 minutes.

Arrange the bananas on top of the filling. Spoon the pineapple over the bananas. Spread with the whipped topping. Sprinkle with the nuts. Arrange the cherries on top. Chill until serving time.

Yield: 10 to 12 servings

Note: To avoid raw eggs that may carry salmonella, use an equivalent amount of pasteurized egg substitute or meringue powder, sometimes sold as powdered egg whites.

Banana Pudding

1 (6-ounce) package vanilla instant pudding mix
1 cup sour cream
1 medium package Cool Whip Whipped Topping
1 package vanilla wafers
4 or 5 bananas
Shredded coconut (optional)

Prepare the pudding mix using the package directions. Combine the pudding, sour cream and whipped topping in a bowl and mix well.

Line the bottom of a dish with vanilla wafers. Layer with $1/3$ of the bananas and pudding mix. Repeat the layers of vanilla wafers, bananas and pudding until all of the pudding is used. Chill until serving time.

Yield: 4 to 6 servings

Note: If you need to increase the amount of banana pudding, use a large package of Cool Whip and add additional vanilla wafers and bananas. This dish is much better if it sits overnight in the refrigerator.

KIND WORDS CAN BE SHORT AND EASY TO SPEAK, BUT

THEIR ECHOES ARE TRULY ENDLESS.

—Mother Theresa

Ooey-Gooey Banana Boat

1 large banana
1 caramel
6 or 10 chocolate caramels, or equivalent chocolate chips
6 to 10 miniature marshmallows
1 graham cracker, crushed

Place the banana on a large piece of heavy-duty foil. Pull back a 1-inch strip of peel from the top of the banana, leaving one end of the strip intact. Loosen the peel on each side of the banana. Cut and remove 3 or 5 alternate pieces of the banana and eat as a snack. Fill the center space of the banana with the caramel. Fill the remaining spaces with equal portions of the chocolate caramels and marshmallows. Cover with the banana peel. Fold the foil to enclose the banana. Place on dying coals for 5 to 10 minutes or until the caramels are melted. Remove with tongs; cool slightly. Open the pouch carefully. Peel the banana. Sprinkle with the crushed graham cracker. Eat with a spoon.

Yield: 1 serving

Note: Cut the foil into a square twice as long as the banana.

ONE CAN NEVER CONSENT TO CREEP WHEN ONE FEELS

AN IMPULSE TO SOAR.

—*Helen Keller*

Red, White and Blue Cobbler

1 (21-ounce) can blueberry pie filling
1 (21-ounce) can cherry pie filling
1 cup flour
1 tablespoon sugar
1¹/2 teaspoons baking powder
¹/2 teaspoon salt
3 tablespoons shortening
¹/2 cup milk

Spread the blueberry pie filling evenly over the bottom of an 8×8-inch glass baking dish. Spread with the cherry pie filling, spreading to the edge. Bake at 400 degrees while preparing the topping. Combine the flour, sugar, baking powder and salt in a bowl and mix well. Cut in the shortening until crumbly. Stir in the milk. Drop by spoonfuls onto the hot pie filling. Bake for 25 to 30 minutes or until browned. Serve with vanilla ice cream.

Yield: 6 servings

Granola Parfaits

2 cups each blueberries, raspberries and strawberries
1 can mandarin oranges, drained
16 ounces vanilla yogurt
2 cups granola
1 small package light whipped topping

Combine the blueberries, raspberries, strawberries and mandarin oranges in a bowl and mix gently. Alternate layers of fruit, yogurt and granola in 4 parfait glasses until all of the ingredients are used. Top with the whipped topping. Chill until serving time.

Yield: 4 servings

Blueberry Oat Dessert Squares

1 cup each chopped walnuts or pecans and quick-cooking oats
1/3 cup sugar
3/4 cup flour
1/2 cup (1 stick) margarine
8 ounces cream cheese, softened
1 1/2 cups confectioners' sugar
1 can blueberry pie filling
1/2 teaspoon cinnamon

Mix the first 4 ingredients in a bowl. Cut in the margarine until crumbly. Reserve 1/2 cup of the walnut mixture. Press the remaining mixture onto the bottom of a 9×9-inch baking pan. Beat the cream cheese in a mixing bowl. Stir in the confectioners' sugar. Spread over the crust. Top with a mixture of the pie filling and cinnamon. Sprinkle with the reserved mixture. Bake at 350 degrees for 20 to 25 minutes.

Yield: 9 servings

Dirt

8 ounces cream cheese, softened
1/4 cup (1/2 stick) margarine, softened
1 cup confectioners' sugar
3 1/2 cups milk
8 ounces Cool Whip Whipped Topping
2 small packages vanilla instant pudding mix
1 package Oreo Chocolate Sandwich Cookies, crushed

Cream the cream cheese, margarine and confectioners' sugar in a mixing bowl. Add the next 3 ingredients and beat at medium speed for 2 minutes. Spread 1/3 of the cookies in the bottom of a clean large clay flowerpot lined with foil. Spoon half the cream cheese mixture into the pot. Layer with half the remaining cookies, the cream cheese mixture and the remaining cookies. Chill.

Eclair Dessert

1 package graham crackers
2 (3-ounce) packages French vanilla instant pudding mix
3¹/₂ cups cold milk
8 ounces Cool Whip Whipped Topping
3 tablespoons butter
2 ounces unsweetened chocolate
3 tablespoons milk
1 tablespoon Karo Light Corn Syrup
1 teaspoon vanilla extract
1¹/₂ cups confectioners' sugar

Butter a 9×13-inch pan. Line the bottom of the pan with graham crackers. Prepare the pudding mix and 3¹/₂ cups milk in a large bowl using the package directions. Add the whipped topping and mix well. Spread half the pudding mixture over the graham crackers. Layer with graham crackers and remaining pudding mixture. Top with graham crackers. Heat the butter and chocolate in a saucepan until melted, stirring constantly. Remove from the heat. Stir in the milk, corn syrup, vanilla and confectioners' sugar. Spread over the top of the layers. Chill until serving time.

Yield: 10 servings

Note: Refrigerate dessert for at least two days before serving.

> *GENIUS IS ONE PERCENT INSPIRATION AND NINETY-NINE*
>
> *PERCENT PERSPIRATION.*
>
> *—Thomas Alva Edison*

Chocolate Peanut Supreme

¹/2 cup chunky peanut butter
¹/3 cup margarine, melted
1¹/2 cups graham cracker crumbs
¹/2 cup sugar
1 (6-ounce) package chocolate instant pudding mix
3 cups cold milk
12 ounces whipped topping
1 cup chopped peanuts

Combine the peanut butter and margarine in a bowl and mix well. Stir in the graham cracker crumbs and sugar. Press onto the bottom of a greased 9×13-inch dish. Prepare the pudding mix and milk using the package directions. Spoon into the prepared dish. Spread with the whipped topping. Sprinkle with the peanuts. Chill, covered, for 1 hour or until set.

Yield: 12 servings

Pumpkin Patch Tartlets

1 quart butter pecan ice cream, softened
³/4 cup canned pumpkin purée
¹/4 cup packed light brown sugar
1 teaspoon cinnamon
12 vanilla wafers
Whipped cream (optional)

Combine the ice cream, pumpkin, brown sugar and cinnamon in a bowl and mix well. Place a paper liner in each of 12 muffin cups. Place a vanilla wafer in the bottom of each muffin cup. Divide the ice cream mixture evenly among the muffin cups. Freeze for several hours. Remove liners and serve tartlets on small plates. Top with whipped cream. Serve immediately.

Yield: 12 servings

Great Pumpkin Dessert

1 (15-ounce) can pumpkin purée
1 (12-ounce) can evaporated milk
3 eggs, or equivalent egg substitute
1 cup sugar, or 1/4 cup fructose
4 teaspoons pumpkin pie spice
1 (2-layer) package yellow cake mix
3/4 cup (1 1/2 sticks) butter or margarine, melted
1 1/2 cups chopped walnuts
8 ounces light cream cheese, softened
1 1/2 cups confectioners' sugar
1 teaspoon vanilla extract
12 ounces light whipped topping

Combine the pumpkin, evaporated milk, eggs, sugar and pumpkin pie spice in a bowl and mix well. Pour into a greased 9×13-inch baking pan. Sprinkle with the cake mix. Drizzle with the butter. Sprinkle the walnuts on top.

Bake at 350 degrees for 1 hour or until a knife inserted in the center comes out clean; cool.

Combine the cream cheese, confectioners' sugar and vanilla in a mixing bowl and beat until smooth. Add the whipped topping and mix well. Spread over the top of the cooled cake. Serve with vanilla ice cream or whipped cream.

Yield: 12 to 16 servings

Note: You may use sugar-free cake mix.

Funnel Cakes

1/4 cup sugar
3 eggs, beaten
1 tablespoon vanilla extract
1/2 teaspoon salt
2 cups milk
3 cups flour
Vegetable oil for frying
Confectioners' sugar

Combine the sugar, eggs, vanilla, salt, milk and flour in a bowl and mix well. Heat 1/2 inch of oil in a skillet to 375 degrees. Drop 1/2 cup of the batter at a time in a swirl pattern into the hot oil using a funnel, making a 6-inch cake. Fry for 3 minutes or until underside is golden brown. Turn the cake over. Fry for 1 minute or until golden brown. Remove to paper towels to drain. Dust with confectioners' sugar. Serve immediately.

Yield: 12 servings

Chinese Chews

16 ounces butterscotch chips
1 (3-ounce) can chow mein noodles
1 cup salted cashews, peanuts or pecans

Melt the butterscotch chips in a large saucepan over low heat. Stir in the noodles and cashews. Drop by spoonfuls onto waxed paper; cool. You may use solar energy to melt the butterscotch chips to make this a fireless food.

Yield: 30 to 36 servings

Note: You may add Cap'N Crunch Peanut Butter Crunch Cereal.

Grandma Annie's Fudge

2 cups sugar
2 tablespoons baking cocoa
1 cup milk
1 teaspoon vanilla extract

Combine the sugar, baking cocoa and milk in a saucepan. Bring to a boil, stirring constantly. Reduce the heat to low. Cook to 234 to 240 degrees on a candy thermometer, soft-ball stage, stirring constantly. Remove from the heat. Add the vanilla and beat until the mixture loses its luster. Pour the mixture onto a buttered plate or shallow pan. Score into squares while warm. Let stand until firm. Cut along score lines and serve.

Yield: 24 servings

Cathedral Candy

12 ounces (2 cups) chocolate chips
1/4 cup (1/2 stick) butter
Dash of salt
5 eggs, beaten
1 (10-ounce) package tinted miniature marshmallows
1 1/2 cups chopped pecans
Confectioners' sugar

Melt the chocolate chips in a double boiler. Add the butter and salt. Cook until the butter is melted, stirring constantly. Stir a small amount of the chocolate mixture into the eggs. Stir the eggs into the chocolate mixture. Cook for 2 minutes, stirring constantly; cool. Add the marshmallows and pecans and mix well. Shape into 4 or 5 logs. Chill, covered, in the refrigerator. Sprinkle with confectioners' sugar. Cut into slices.

Yield: 24 servings

Daisy's Taffy

2 cups sugar
1/4 cup vinegar
1/2 cup light corn syrup
3/4 cup water

Combine the sugar, vinegar, corn syrup and water in a saucepan. Bring to a simmer, stirring constantly. Simmer until the sugar is dissolved, stirring constantly. Cook to 270 to 290 degrees on a candy thermometer, soft-crack stage; do not stir. Pour onto a well-greased surface; cool. Pull with well-greased hands until white. Cut into bite-size pieces.

Yield: 12 to 15 servings

Spiced Pecans

1 egg white
1 teaspoon water
1 pound pecan halves
1/2 cup sugar
1/4 teaspoon salt
1/2 teaspoon cinnamon

Beat the egg white and water in a mixing bowl until fluffy. Add the pecans, tossing to coat. Combine the sugar, salt and cinnamon in a large bowl and mix well. Add the pecans, stirring to coat. Arrange in a single layer on a baking sheet. Bake at 225 degrees for 1 hour, turning every 15 minutes.

Yield: 20 servings

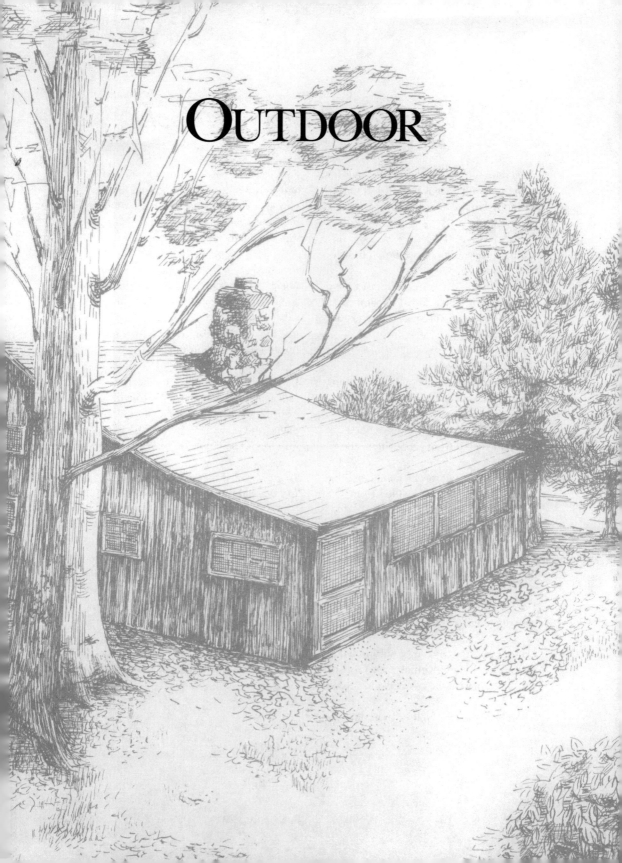

OUTDOOR

Hints for Outdoor Cooks

Vegetables such as celery, carrots, radishes, cabbage, and lettuce will stay fresh longer if wrapped in foil and several layers of brown paper.

A little vinegar will remove onion or fish odor from a skillet.

A little dab of butter added to oatmeal while it's cooking will make the pot easier to clean.

Drop a small pat of butter or one tablespoon of vegetable oil into spaghetti water to prevent it from boiling over.

Sprinkle a few drops of water on sliced bacon to keep it from shriveling in the pan.

Add a pinch of salt to water when boiling a cracked egg to prevent whites from running out.

To keep salt and pepper shakers from spilling while traveling, place a piece of plastic wrap under the lid.

Use lids whenever possible to cut down on cooking time.

Quarter-inch dowels can be substituted for thin sticks (1 inch for thick sticks) for stick cookery. They can be cleaned and reused.

A can or bottle may be used as a rolling pin.

Eggs can be removed from the shell whole and stored in a small plastic (size of an olive jar) jar with a lid. The eggs will not break and can be poured out one at a time when needed.

Do not spray nonstick cooking spray on a hot skillet or near coals or open flame. The spray can ignite causing the can to explode.

Use fingernail polish to mark foil dinners. It will not burn off in the coals.

When broiling, do not cook meats or other foods directly on discarded refrigerator or stove shelves. Some of these are cadmium-plated and may cause violent illness. Cover with foil for safe use.

To give broiled meats a barbecue flavor, sprinkle lightly with instant coffee.

To remove single strips of sliced bacon from a package, roll the package tightly. The strips will come off easily.

When heating food in its own can, open the can first to release steam and prevent the can from exploding.

A piece of apple or orange inside a covered container of brown sugar will keep it soft.

Campsite Stew

1 pound ground beef
1/2 cup chopped onion
3 large potatoes, peeled and chopped (about 3 cups)
1 (16-ounce) can cream-style corn
1 can condensed beef broth
1 teaspoon salt
Dash of pepper

Brown the ground beef with the onion in a large skillet, stirring until crumbly; drain. Add the potatoes, corn, broth, salt and pepper and mix well. Reduce the heat to low. Cook, covered, for 20 to 25 minutes, stirring occasionally. Serve immediately.

Yield: 4 servings

Easy Supper Dish

8 ounces ground beef
Chopped onion to taste
1 teaspoon salt
1/2 teaspoon pepper
1 cup uncooked macaroni
2 cups tomato juice
1 cup (4 ounces) shredded Cheddar cheese

Brown the ground beef in a skillet, stirring until crumbly; drain. Add the onion, salt and pepper and mix well. Stir in the macaroni and tomato juice. Bring to a boil. Reduce the heat to low. Cook for 15 to 30 minutes or until the macaroni is tender, stirring occasionally. Sprinkle with the cheese. Cook, covered, until the cheese is melted.

Yield: 4 servings

Phoebe's Beans

5 to 7 slices bacon
1 medium onion, chopped
1 pound ground beef
1 (28-ounce) can baked beans
1 can stewed tomatoes
1/2 cup barbecue sauce
1 tablespoon brown sugar
2 tablespoons spicy mustard
1 teaspoon hot pepper sauce

Chop the bacon. Cook the bacon in a large saucepan until crisp, stirring occasionally. Remove to paper towels using a slotted spoon. Brown the onion in the bacon drippings, stirring frequently. Add the ground beef. Cook until browned and crumbly, stirring frequently; drain. Add the beans, tomatoes, barbecue sauce, brown sugar, mustard and hot pepper sauce and mix well. Simmer for 15 to 29 minutes, stirring occasionally. Sprinkle with the bacon and serve.

Yield: 6 to 8 servings

Ham Yams

4 yams
1 cup chopped ham
1 cup pineapple chunks
1/3 cup packed brown sugar
1/4 cup miniature marshmallows

Cut the yams lengthwise into halves. Scoop out the pulp, leaving the shells intact. Combine the ham, pineapple and brown sugar in a bowl and mix well. Spoon equal portions of the mixture into the yams. Close the yams and wrap securely in foil. Arrange on a wire rack 2 to 3 inches above the coals or wrap in insulated foil and place directly on the coals. Cook for 30 to 45 minutes per side. Unwrap the yams carefully. Place a few marshmallows inside the yams and reassemble the packet. Let stand for a few minutes until the marshmallows are melted.

Yield: 4 servings

IN MATTERS OF STYLE, SWIM WITH THE CURRENT; IN

MATTERS OF PRINCIPLE, STAND LIKE A ROCK.

—Thomas Jefferson

Mustard Barbecue Sauce

2 cups prepared mustard
1 cup mayonnaise
1/3 cup ketchup
2 tablespoons sugar
2 tablespoons Worcestershire sauce
1 teaspoon Kitchen Bouquet
1/2 teaspoon seasoned salt
1/4 teaspoon pepper
1/4 cup (1/2 stick) butter or margarine
1/2 cup water
1/4 teaspoon liquid smoke (optional)

Combine the mustard, mayonnaise, ketchup, sugar, Worcestershire sauce, Kitchen Bouquet, seasoned salt, pepper, butter, water and liquid smoke in a saucepan and mix well. Bring to a boil over high heat, stirring frequently. Reduce the heat to medium. Cook for 10 minutes, stirring occasionally. Use to baste chicken, pork chops, ribs or turkey drumsticks.

Yield: (about) 5 1/3 cups

Grilled Herbed Potatoes

3 or 4 small red potatoes (about 2 inches in diameter), scrubbed
1 tablespoon canola oil
Garlic salt to taste
Lemon pepper to taste
1 large sprig of fresh basil, thyme or other herb

Arrange the potatoes on a double-wide piece of heavy-duty foil. Coat the potatoes with the canola oil. Sprinkle with garlic salt and lemon pepper. Top with a basil sprig. Fold the foil to enclose the potatoes. Place directly on medium coals. Cook for 30 to 40 minutes or until the potatoes are tender and browned, turning once or twice. You may cook the potatoes on the bottom rack of a gas grill over low heat.

Yield: 1 serving

Note: You may substitute white potatoes for the red potatoes. Cut large potatoes into 2-inch pieces. Recipe may be easily doubled or tripled.

LEADERSHIP SHOULD BE BORN OUT OF THE UNDERSTANDING

OF THE NEEDS OF THOSE WHO WOULD BE AFFECTED BY IT.

—Marian Anderson

Jan's Scrambled Eggs

1/2 cup thinly sliced Vidalia onion
1 cup sliced asparagus
Sliced carrots (optional)
2 tablespoons butter or margarine
1/2 cup sliced mushrooms
8 medium to large eggs
5 slices cheese, torn
Chopped cooked ham, bacon or sausage (optional)

Sauté the onion, asparagus and carrots in the butter in a large skillet just until tender. Add the mushrooms. Sauté just until tender. Combine the eggs, cheese and ham in a bowl and mix well. Add to the mushroom mixture. Cook for 6 minutes or until the eggs are fluffy, stirring constantly.

Yield: 2 or 3 servings

Note: I eat my scrambled eggs with a hot dog. You may notice that I believe in throwing in everything and the kitchen sink.

Casualty

8 ounces bacon
1 can sliced potatoes, drained
6 to 8 eggs
Milk (optional)

Cut the bacon into small pieces. Cook the bacon in a skillet until almost done, stirring frequently. Add the potatoes. Cook until the potatoes are browned, stirring frequently. Beat the eggs and a small amount of milk in a bowl. Add to the bacon mixture. Cook until the eggs are fluffy, stirring constantly.

Yield: 2 or 3 servings

Note: Great for camping.

YOU GAIN STRENGTH, COURAGE AND CONFIDENCE BY EVERY EXPERIENCE IN WHICH YOU REALLY STOP TO LOOK FEAR IN THE FACE. YOU MUST DO THE THINGS YOU THINK YOU CANNOT DO.

—Eleanor Roosevelt

Chocolate Chip Pancakes

1¹/₂ cups flour
1 teaspoon salt
3 tablespoons sugar
1³/₄ teaspoons baking powder
2 eggs
3 tablespoons butter, melted
1 cup milk
Chocolate chips to taste

Sift the flour, salt, sugar and baking powder into a bowl. Add the eggs, butter and milk and mix well. Pour ¹/₄ cup at a time onto a hot, lightly greased griddle or skillet. Sprinkle with chocolate chips. Cook until bubbles appear on the surface and the underside is golden brown. Turn the pancake. Cook until golden brown. Serve with butter and syrup.

Yield: 6 to 8 servings

Note: You may substitute "M&M's" Chocolate Candies, peanut butter chips, or white chocolate chips for the chocolate chips.

WHEN BEATING EGG WHITES FOR MERINGUE, MAKE

ABSOLUTELY SURE THE BOWL AND BEATERS

ARE DRY AND THERE IS NOT ONE SPECK OF YELLOW

YOLK OR IT WILL BE RUINED.

Banana Barges

Bananas
Chocolate chips (chopped)
Strawberry jelly
Miniature marshmallows
Crushed pineapple
Finely chopped nuts

Cut a slit in each banana or peel back a strip from the top of each banana. Stuff each banana with chocolate chips, strawberry jelly, marshmallows, pineapple and nuts. Wrap securely in heavy-duty foil. Place on hot coals. Cook for 5 minutes or until the chocolate and marshmallows are melted.

Yield: variable

S'More Trail Mix

2 cups honey graham cereal
1 cup miniature marshmallows
1 cup peanuts
1/2 cup (3 ounces) semisweet chocolate chips
1/2 cup raisins

Combine the cereal, marshmallows, peanuts, chocolate chips and raisins in a sealable plastic bag and shake to mix. Store in the plastic bag or a tightly covered container.

Yield: (about) 5 cups

Equivalents

3 teaspoons	1 tablespoon	4 cups	1 quart
4 tablespoons	1/4 cup	4 quarts	1 gallon
5 1/3 tablespoons	1/3 cup	8 quarts	1 peck
8 tablespoons	1/2 cup	4 pecks	1 bushel
10 2/3 tablespoons	2/3 cup	16 ounces	1 pound
12 tablespoons	3/4 cup	32 ounces	1 quart
16 tablespoons	1 cup	8 ounces liquid	1 cup
2 cups	1 pint	1 ounce liquid	2 tablespoons

(For liquid and dry measurements, use standard measuring spoons and cups.
All measurements are level.)

Cornmeal
1 pound . . . . .3 cups

Cheese, American
1 pound . . . . .2 2/3 cups cubed

Sugar
1 pound brown . . . . .2 1/2 cups
1 pound granulated . . . . .2 cups
1 pound confectioners . . . . .3 1/2 cups

Eggs
1 egg . . . . .4 tablespoons liquid
4 to 5 whole . . . . .1 cup
7 to 9 whites . . . . .1 cup
12 to 14 yolks . . . . .1 cup

Cracker Crumbs
23 soda crackers . . . . .1 cup
15 graham crackers . . . . .1 cup

Shortening or Butter
1 pound . . . . .2 cups

Flour
1 pound all-purpose . . . . .4 cups
1 pound cake . . . . .4 1/2 cups
1 pound graham . . . . .3 1/2 cups

Lemons, Juice
1 medium . . . . .2 to 3 tablespoons
5 to 8 medium . . . . .1 cup

Lemons, Zest
1 lemon . . . . .1 tablespoon grated

Oranges, Juice
1 medium . . . . .2 to 3 tablespoons
3 to 4 medium . . . . .1 cup

Oranges, Zest
1 orange . . . . .2 tablespoons grated

Gelatin
3 1/4 ounce package . . . . .1/2 cup
  flavored
1/4 ounce package . . . . .1 tablespoon
  unflavored

Substitutions

For these	You may use these
1 whole egg, for thickening or baking	2 egg yolks, or 2 tablespoons dried whole egg plus $2^1/2$ tablespoons water
1 cup butter or margarine or shortening	$7/8$ cup lard, or rendered fat, with $1/2$ teaspoon salt, or 1 cup hydrogenated fat (cooking fat sold under brand name) with $1/2$ teaspoon salt
1 square (ounce) chocolate	3 or 4 tablespoons cocoa plus $1/2$ tablespoon fat
Sweet milk and baking powder, for baking	Equal amount of sour milk plus $1/2$ teaspoon baking soda per cup (each half teaspoon baking soda with 1 cup sour milk takes the place of 2 teaspoons baking powder and 1 cup sweet milk)
1 cup sour milk, for baking	1 cup sweet milk mixed with one of the following: 1 tablespoon vinegar, 1 tablespoon lemon juice, or $1^3/4$ teaspoons cream of tartar
1 cup whole milk	$1/2$ cup evaporated milk plus $1/2$ cup water, 4 tablespoons dry whole milk plus 1 cup water, or 4 tablespoons nonfat dry milk plus 2 teaspoons table fat and 1 cup water
1 cup skim milk	4 tablespoons nonfat dry milk plus 1 cup water
1 tablespoon flour, for thickening	$1/2$ teaspoon cornstarch, potato starch, rice starch, or arrowroot starch, or 1 tablespoon granulated tapioca
1 cup cake flour, for baking	$7/8$ cup all-purpose flour
1 cup all-purpose flour, for baking breads	Up to $1/2$ cup bran, whole wheat flour, or cornmeal plus enough all-purpose flour to fill cup

Contributors

Maddie Adams
Bev Ball
Alma Barnes
Marlo Barnhart
Amanda Beal
April Beal
Sheila Beal
Brenda Beam
Gwen Blacklin
Dana T. Bostwick
Mary Bourdeau
Linda Bucher
Rachel Butts
Janice Carper
Mary Kelsea Casto
Betty K. Chapman
Robin Clem
Nicole Conde
Dee Covey
Marguerite E. Cyr
Cathy Dalke
Bonnie DeBoard
Breanne DeGrave
Jeanne DeGrave
Lisa DeGrave
Nicole DeGrave
Ora Dixon
Jessica Dodson
Elaine Dorosh
Glenora Faupel
Morgan Fitkin

Peyton Fitkin
Erma Foltz
Molly Forrest
Becky Franks
Florida Fritz
Earlene Garnitz
Karen L. Garrett
Susan Garrett
Kayla Githens
Shonda Githens
Megan Givens
Ciara Hall
Jenae Hanes
Lisa Hileman
Chloe Housden
Mary Ann Jenkins
Kathy Jewell
April Johnson
Sandy Jones
Mary Lange Kalin
Mary Lehman
Janice Leonard
Shelbi Lerch
Candy Maddalena
Lois Marbert
Eleanor (Babe) McDaniel
Cescily Metzgar
Aili Miller
Christi Miller
Colleen Miller
Frances Kief Newbraugh

Nancy S. Palmer
Sharon L. Palmer
Sally Pepper, D.V.M.
Sue Pownall
Becky Pyne
Nancy Reed
Melissa Reid
Betty Lou Rinn
Rose Rohrbaugh
Frances M. Russ
Ann Ryan
Megan Ryan
Rachel Ryan
Ronnie Ryan
Alice S. Shell
Fran Shockey
Katlyn Simmons
Denise Sirk
Wilma L. Smith
Georgia Taylor
Mary Lou Thompson
Loretta Thornhill
Jeanne M. Vollmer
Sharon Wiercioch
Carolyn Wilson
Katie Wilson
Patricia Witmer
Eva Woolridge
LeAnna Young
Ann Zerull
Lisa Zerull

Gold Award Scholarship Fund

Established in 1977 with an initial contribution from Eva Woolridge, the Girl Scouts of Shawnee Council Girl Scout Gold Award Scholarship Fund provides scholarships each year in recognition of outstanding achievements in the areas of leadership, service, and commitment to the principles and ideals of Girl Scouting. Financial need is not a part of the criteria used in awarding these scholarships.

Awarded in 1997-1998

Amy Reid—Hagerstown Business College
Kari Sargent—Lord Fairfax . Community College
Terina Westmeyer

Awarded in 1998-1999

Melinda Baldwin—University of Virginia at Wise
Sandra Bostwick—Shepherd College
Nicole Braithwaite— Shenandoah University
Melissa Coffelt—Lord Fairfax Community College
Kelly Foster—Lord Fairfax Community College
Kimberly Foster—Lord Fairfax Community College
Jocelyn Shaffer—Shenandoah University

Awarded in 1999-2000

Note: All applications presented during this year were carried to the 2000-2001 year for consideration.

Awarded in 2000–2001

Anna Barvir—College of Notre Dame of Maryland
Jennifer Cameron—Eastern Mennonite University
Amy Campbell—Hagerstown Community College
Carrie Chapman—Lord Fairfax Community College
Lisa DeGrave—Shepherd College
Raine Johnson—Shepherd College
Erin Sytsma—College of William and Mary
Valarie Taylor—Emory & Henry College

Awarded in 2001–2002

Sylvia Barvir—Hagerstown Community College
Carrie Chapman—Lord Fairfax Community College
Nicole Clem—Lord Fairfax Community College
Jenna Garrett—Shepherd College
Kelly Jo Hinkle—Shepherd College
Stacey Jones—Oakbridge Academy of Arts
Kathryn Norman—Lord Fairfax Community College

Gold Award Recipients

1981
Denise Cooley

1982
Carol Weir
Janet Williams

1985
Valentina Daily
Cheryl Ann Litten
Edwina Orndorff
Gayle Tisinger

1986
Alberta Coffman
Stacey Eye
Mary Frances Irvin
Brenda Jenkins
Julie McClanahan

1987
Wendy Clem
Tammy Hopcraft
Amy Jenkins
Tammy Jenkins
Dawn Rinker

1988
Jenny Allen
Donna J. Bowman
Brenda Dorsch
Lori Garrett
Jenny Gilpin
Amy Johnson
Pam A. Miller
Kara Neitzey
Sharon Palmer
Liz Sechler
Dorothy Sellers
Aney Stoner

1989
Melissa Freeman
Renée Kuykendall
April Johnson
Lori Mongold
Terra Staley

1990
Lea Barrow
Michelle Clark
Amy Daniels
Holly Lam
Debbie Miller
Michele Moyer
Stacey Stottlemyer
Karen Tucker
Diane Welch

1991
Jennifer Benzie
Jennifer Carr
Julia Shaw

1992
Annette Brown
Nicole DeGrave
Margaret Lee
Holly Painter
Melissa Penn
Marla Ryan
Nikki Stevenson

1993
Rebecca Adams
Refa Blakely
Bonnie Cheshire
Gail Davis
Pat Grimes
Julie Heath
Mindee Hite
Terry LaFollette
Kathryn Lawler
Lisa Snyder
Anita Wright

1994

Jean Beydler
Gesina Campuzano
Crystal Carr
Carrie Clise
Ruth Ann Dermer
Amy Dolly
Laura James
Jennifer Estep
Kathryn George
Kristina George
Elizabeth Johnson
Allison Lampton
Seiglinde Leahy
Shonda Lucas
Elizabeth Miller
Leanne Richards
Beth Van Why
Meredith Zirkle

1995

Jamie Heishman
Kristina Justice
Julie Faye Kimbrill
Emily Kirkland
Erynn Lohman
Sarah McKee
Bethany Mercer
Elizabeth Nesselrodt
Melanie Richards
Rhonalee Russell
Sarah Skiles
Stephanie Smith

Marsha Sollenberger
Kelly Staley
Melanie Walters
Heather Woodman

1996

April Brill
Lauren Burton
Maneika Campuzano
Elizabeth Dalton
Stacey Dayton
Jessica Estep
Diane Grimes
Tiffany Helsley
Kristine Hummel
Brenda Johnson
Jennifer Lidie
Megan Long
Lynell Joy McBride
Janelle Moyer
Amanda Rogers
Kari Sargent
Mary Shrout
Amy Stultz
Mary Suddath

1997

Stephanie Bailes
Melinda Baldwin
Mary Bartlett
Anne Bowerman
Sarah Bowyer
Kelley Burke
Becky Costello
Sarah Drosseleyer
Spring Mariah Fertig
Johanna Fox
Katheryn Hockman
Megan Hoffman
Erica Huston
Elizabeth Hutson
Crystal Kitts
Tiffany Kitts
Jennifer Lee
Holly Lohr
Jenna Mallery
Jessica Monish
Heather Moorehead
Katie Nesselrodt
Lisa Seal
Sara Shaw
Andrea Pleasant
Heather Winfield
Samantha Zeznanski

1998

Sandra Bostwick
Rebecca Breeden
Nicole Braithwaite
Christy Carter
Heather Chamblin
Crystal Crist
Julia Crowell
Kelli Beth Davis
Heather Fauble
Kelly Foster
Kim Foster
Rachel Gallaway
Jennifer Gorman
Jennell Hedges
Virginia Hudson
Melanie Huston
Adrienne Kesner
Tiffany Kitts
April Mack
Erin Mickey
Danielle Miller
Crystal Nave
Kimberly Painter
Lynn Phillips
Amy Reid
Jocelyn Shaffer
Stephanie Smith
Amanda Story
Patti Suddath
Samantha Twigg
Terina Westmeyer
Betsy Whetzel

1999

Angela Adams
Anna Barvir
Mary Beth Blair
Jennifer Cameron
Carrie Chapman
Melissa Coffelt
Lisa DeGrave
LaAngel Fredman
Mindy Henderson
Jennifer Hodgson
Megan Huston
Rebekah Jaswa
Anna Jensen
Jodi Moats
Christine Mongold
Katheryn Norman
Amy O'Brien
Michelle Rogers
Jeanette Shaffer
Dixie Stroop
Erin Sytsma
Megan Thomas
Jenna Workman

2000

Amy Campbell
Sara Cline
Raine Johnson
Beth Moyer
Joy Pereira
Valarie Taylor
Angel Wilkins

2001

Sylvia Barvir
Lynnette Bolinger
Nicole Clem
Jenna Garrett
Kelly Jo Hinkle
Stacey Jones
Patricia Mitchell
Katie Pehowski
Megan Stephens
Sarah Taylor
Stephanie Taylor
Sita Zarcufsky

2002

Erin Ebersole
Heather Ebersole
Molly Henderson
Callie Long
Laura Mickey

Index

141

Generations Of Cooking

Girl Scouts of Shawnee Council, Inc.
153 McMillan Court
Martinsburg, West Virginia 25401
304-263-8833

YOUR ORDER	QUANTITY	TOTAL
Generations Of Cooking at $16.00 per book		$
West Virginia residents add $.96 sales tax per book		$
Postage and handling at $2.00 per book		$
	TOTAL	$

Name _____

Address _____

City _____ State _____ Zip _____

Telephone _____

Method of Payment: [   ] American Express   [   ] Discover
[   ] MasterCard   [   ] VISA
[   ] Check payable to Girl Scouts of Shawnee Council, Inc.

Account Number _____ Expiration Date _____

Signature _____

Photocopies will be accepted.